Old Musical Instruments

René Clemencic

OCTOPUS BOOKS

Acknowledgments

This edition first published 1973 by
OCTOPUS BOOKS LIMITED
59 Grosvenor Street, London W1

ISBN 0 7064 0057 7

© 1968 George Weidenfeld & Nicolson Ltd
Translated by David Hermges

Produced by Mandarin Publishers Limited
77a Marble Road, North Point, Hong Kong
and printed in Hong Kong

The author and publishers wish to thank the authorities of the following museums and collections, by whose kind permission the illustrations are reproduced: AMSTERDAM, Rijksmuseum, 75; BERLIN, Staatliches Institut für Musikforschung, 82, 111; BOSTON, Museum of Fine Arts, 30 (Gift of William Lindsey in memory of his daughter Mrs Leslie Lindsey), 121; BRUSSELS, Conservatoire Royal de Musique, 47, 48, 49, 61, 117; COPENHAGEN, Carl Claudius' Musikhistoriske Samling, 74, 98; Musikhistorisk Museum, 96; Rosenborg Castle, 72; THE HAGUE, Gemeentemuseum, 50, 92, 108, 119; HAMBURG, Kunsthalle, 9; KREMSMÜNSTER Abbey, 38; LEIPZIG, Karl-Marx-University, 5, 11; LONDON, Benton Fletcher Collection of Early Keyboard Instruments, Fenton House, Hampstead, 99; British Museum, 28, 93; Courtauld Institute of Art (Roger Fry Collection), 123; National Gallery, 68; Royal College of Music, 94; Victoria & Albert Museum (Crown copyright), 8, 20, 25, 27, 29, 32, 33, 40, 44, 62, 76, 83; MUNICH, Bayerisches Nationalmuseum, 54; Deutsches Museum, 95, 101, 105; Städtische Musikinstrumentensammlung, 110; NEW YORK, Metropolitan Museum of Art, 102 (Gift of Mr and Mrs William H. Herriman, 1911); OXFORD, Ashmolean Museum, 84, 116; PARIS, Bibliothéque Nationale, 6, 43; Conservatoire Nationale de Musique, 58, 66, 67, 71, 73, 89, 91, 104, 112; Musée du Louvre, 57; SALEM, Mass., Essex Institute, 107; STOCKHOLM, Musikhistoriska Museet, 78–81; VIENNA, Bildarchiv der öst. Nationalbibliothek, 10, 16, 31, 34, 39, 52, 56, 60, 77, 86, 106; Gesellschaft der Musikfreunde, 22; Heeresgeschichtliches Museum, 122; Kunsthistorisches Museum, 1, 7, 12, 13, 14, 15, 35, 36, 37, 41, 42, 46, 51, 55, 70, 87, 88, 118, 120; Öst. Museum für angewandte Kunst, 18, 100; René Clemencic collection, 3, 4, 19, 21, 24, 26, 45, 63, 69, 97, 103, 109, 113, 114, 115; Dr Walther Clemencic collection, 2; Wolfgang Hofstätter collection, 85; Roderich von Roy collection, 65; YALE University, Bell Skinner Collection, 59.

Photographs were supplied by: Bärenreiter Bildarchiv, 23; Werner Forman, 13, 14, 15, 18, 21, 24, 26, 53, 55, 63, 69, 85, 87, 88, 103, 109, 113, 114, 115, 120; Giraudon, 57; Claus Hansmann, 95, 101, 105, 110; Kunsthistorisches Museum, 22; Derrick Witty, 29, 32, 99; and other objects in the collections of the author and Dr Walther Clemencic were photographed by Martin Schaub and Franz-Xaver Schwarzenberger.

The author is particularly indebted to the catalogues of the Collection of Musical Instruments of the Vienna Kunsthistorisches Museum by Schlosser, and by Luithlen and Wegerer, and to the catalogues of the other collections containing instruments described in this book.

Preceding page:
(From left to right) Baryton by Jacques Sainprae, Berlin, c. 1720; Hurdy-gurdy, French, 18th century; Lute with ivory back, Italian?, 17th century; Octave spinet, Italian, c. 1600. Victoria and Albert Museum, London.

Contents

Introduction

THERE IS A MYSTERIOUS MAGIC about sound. Consciously or unconsciously it is assumed to be the most direct means of expression of gods, spirits, men and even inanimate objects. Something hidden is communicated by sound – whether proclamation, warning or enticement. We are brought into contact with its essence. Nothing affects us so immediately, perhaps making us change our mind, as sound. On the other hand nothing can be more disturbing to our ears than unfamiliar sounds. The evocative power of aural enchantment is retained to this day in certain instrumental sounds. Ponderous brass passages induce instant solemnity; clarion trumpet calls arouse aggressive instincts; the wondrous notes of an organ imply devotion; a jazz-drummer's 'break' whips the emotions; a prolonged flourish of trombones conjures up a vision of the Last Judgment.

Among the primitive tribes of Oceania, Africa and Australasia, whose way of life reproduces to a certain extent the conditions prevailing in the early days of human society, special importance is attached – apart from the human voice – to wind instruments and to the so-called idiophones. Curt Sachs, in his *History of Musical Instruments,* describes the latter group of instruments as those 'made of naturally sonorous materials not needing any additional tension as do strings or drumskins'. Wind instruments are in direct contact with the mysterious, invisible air that surrounds us. A wind player is more intimately linked with his instrument than the player of other instruments since he forms the sounds with his own breath. In this way Man too can provide the breath of life – for musical existence. The flute, that wind instrument *par excellence* (whose name derives from the Latin *flatus* = breath, blowing, breeze), is always one whose

> … sound of magic has the power
> To guard us safe in death's dread hour

as the Prince Tamino sings in Mozart's opera *The Magic Flute.*

The idiophones 'speak' on their own, revealing their hidden voice by mere striking or shaking without any exceptional preparations normally being necessary. The material world starts to sound when it is set into vibration or motion. Plutarch, describing the ancient Egyptian *sistrum*, says 'it shows that things should constantly be in a state of motion. When they

2   The Sirens symbolize the forces of destruction unleashed by evil sounds. Whoever heeds their infatuating enticements must perish.

1   *(opposite)* Allegory of Vanity by Leonhard Bramer (1596–1674), a follower of Rembrandt. Secular music was often regarded as symbolizing the vanity of this world. The musician is playing a theorbo, and on the right of the picture there are a lute, two violins, a cittern, a flute and a bass viol.

3 The Egyptian *sistrum,* an idiophone sounded by rattling, is intended to show people that the world, faced with the constant threat of death, has to be constantly shaken out of its lethargy.

4 Membranophones have always had magical associations with death. The skins were looked on as the singing relics of a living being. Even in this Baroque engraving of a Dance of Death something of the mystique is retained.

slumber or cease to move then they should be awakened and kept in vibration. They [the Egyptians] believe that with the *sistrum* they can ward off Typhon, and thus indicate that the induction of movement preserves Nature from destruction and sets it going again.'

Both the membranophones (drums, etc.) and the chordophones (string instruments) appear to be of somewhat less antiquity. They are first found in early neolithic days. Contact with the instrument is, in these groups, nothing like as direct as it is in the case of aerophones (wind instruments), and their sonorous material can only be made to sound after special treatment and preparation. The instrument, regarded simply as a utensil for doing something, intervenes increasingly between man and his world, and the world becomes more and more the setting for *homo faber,* the artisan. This is exactly what the 'existentialist' philosopher Martin Heidegger was getting at when he said: 'A tool is essentially only "something to…"'.

The disembodiment inherent in the production of 'organized sounds' leads finally to the invention of western keyboard instruments on which the player is separated by mechanism from the actual sound-producing apparatus and often only retains 'stop-go' powers. Whereas in very early times the shape of the instruments and their sound had symbolic and magical implications, later on instruments came to be judged mainly for the aesthetic values of their form and sonority, although the element of magic is never entirely discarded.

It is just as wrong to talk about the 'development of musical instruments' as it is to talk about the 'development' of music, painting, sculpture or any other art. The naïve nineteenth-century belief that everything new represented progress is quite out of place here. Every epoch, every civilization creates its own instruments – in the widest sense of the term – which are adequate for the sounds it wants to produce. (There is an obvious parallel here with the various sorts of singing that have been regarded as ideal at different times.) Only in the case of keyboard instruments is it possible to speak, though with considerable reservations, of an improvement in the strictly mechanical sense. This 'improvement', though, is generally accompanied by alterations in playing technique, as well as by a deterioration in tonal characteristics, both of which spoil the final result.

In this book an attempt is made to relate as closely as possible the outward characteristics of old musical instruments with the art and literature of the relevant period. The author has limited his choice, however, to western instruments dating from High Renaissance to Classicist times. Too few instruments made prior to 1500 have survived to permit anything like satisfactory commentary; and instruments constructed after the middle of the nineteenth century are of insufficient aesthetic interest.

High Renaissance

5 Italian Renaissance positive organ of classical proportions. The base is decorated with biblical scenes and the top with the arms of the Rovere family, from which came the Renaissance Pope Julius II.

AN UNHEARD WEALTH OF TONAL COLOUR greets us, a world of rich diversity, beside which our modern orchestral palette appears poverty-stricken. At this time there was a whole range of plucked and bowed string instruments, penetrating double-reed instruments, sweet sounding instruments of the flute family, instruments with cupped mouthpieces, some as resounding as the trumpet, others – like the trombone and the cornett – as gentle as the human voice. And all of these instruments existed in various sizes, often in whole 'families'.

This habit of building instruments in families was very characteristic of the High Renaissance and the subsequent Mannerist periods. The tendency diminished in Baroque times. Subsequently it was only the string section of the classical, romantic and modern orchestra which perpetuated the system. The addiction to families of instruments, a trend which became apparent towards the end of the fifteenth century, was not just a whim of the makers. Rather did it spring from a general desire for the homogeneous sound required by the new musical style. Whereas medieval polyphony implied simultaneous, artfully co-ordinated integration of different melodic strains, often with different rhythms and even sung in different languages, ever since the fifteenth century the parts were expected to approach more closely and blend with one another. Each voice acquired an individual status of its own on the basis of democratic equality. Henceforth homogeneity was the aim. In practice, of course, the principle was disregarded fairly frequently either because of archaisms in composing technique or because the performance needed tonal variety. There was another reason for homogeneity too, though: a homogeneous ensemble is better suited for realizing chords than an ensemble where each voice has a different 'colour'. The coincidence of sounds of different pitch in medieval music was sporadic and often unintentional. Nevertheless it was governed by certain rules whose only function was not to spoil the melodic line until, as from the fifteenth century, stress began to be laid on the inherent virtues of harmony. Another, final, advantage of extending the families of instruments was that clearly differentiated musical space was made available, on top and below, compared with the almost indeterminate middle region favoured in medieval days. This exciting new spacial expansion can be paralleled in the painting of the same period. Music was to a certain extent humanized and brought down to earth, its feet firmly weighted in the bass line.

The rapidly increasing importance of KEYBOARD INSTRUMENTS can be traced to the same overall attitude: polyphonic play is henceforth possible not just on related instruments but on one and the same instrument comprising the whole family.

That a stringed instrument (especially the psaltery), normally plucked by finger-tip or plectrum, could be mechanized by means of a levered key had been recognized since the fourteenth century. Various shapes are possible for the instrument. If it is rectangular, pentagonal or approximately trapezoidal (for which the general name is virginal or spinet) then the strings run parallel to the keyboard or at a slight angle to it; if the strings run straight away from the keyboard – which is at the short end, so to speak – and give the whole a wing-like shape then it should be referred to as a harpsichord [figure 6].

The Victoria and Albert Museum in London has the oldest HARPSICHORD that can be definitely dated. In the sixteenth century the Italians led the world in making plucked string keyboard instruments, and the harpsichord made in 1521 by Hieronymus of Bologna is a fully mature instrument in every respect. The classically beautiful wing shape is chosen for purely functional reasons and represents the harmonious curve of the various string lengths. The soundboard has a sound-hole with ornamental rosette. The front end of the light-coloured keys is carved and the keyboard sides are also decorated [figure 8]. The wording on the ornamental keyboard cover draws attention to the cosmic, Orphean powers of harmony:

ASPICITE VT TRAHITVR SVAVI MODVLAMINE VOCIS QVICQVID HABENT AER SIDERA TERRA FRETUM
(Behold how everything contained in air, heaven, earth and sea is moved by the sweet sound of melody!)

Right through until its disappearance in the eighteenth century the Italian harpsichord retained this classical shape. Afterwards the first pianofortes kept the tradition alive. The usual German word for a 'grand' piano is still *Flügel* (= wing). This continuity was characteristic for Italy, although in other countries all sorts of changes were made.

The CLAVICHORD represents another method of mechanizing a stringed instrument. The strings are struck by metal 'tangents' (small metal blades fixed at the far end of the key-levers). Since these tangents are an integral part of the keys they do not fall back into place like the quills of a harpsichord or the hammers of a piano. And so when a key is depressed in playing, the tangent also divides the vibrating length of the string. Depending on the point where contact is made the note produced can vary. The sound is very delicate but is also very susceptible to modulation

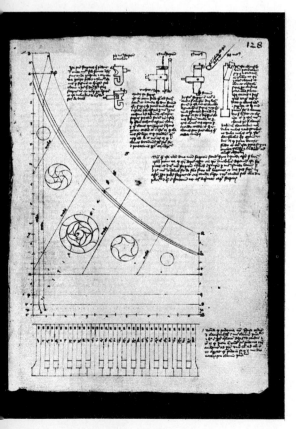

6 The oldest known constructional plan for a harpsichord by Henricus Arnault of Zwolle (c. 1435). The wing-like shape is derived naturally from the way the strings are arranged according to their length. The use of several sound-holes was soon abandoned.

8 Like most Italian harpsichords this, the oldest example known, is made of cypress wood. The instrument proper is kept in a richly decorated outer case – another typical Italian feature.

9 Thanks to its low cost and its delicate tone the clavichord was one of the most popular instruments for use in the home. Engraving by the Flemish artist J. C. Vermeijen (1500–59).

because of the direct pressure exercised by the player's finger. The instrument's subtlety of touch and low initial cost (resulting from the simplicity of its construction) made it popular for instruction and exercise. Paulus Behaim, a citizen of Nuremberg, noted in his account-book for 1567: 'On 9 November sent my son to the organist that he might learn touch of the clavichord.'

The instrument has clearly been in use since the latter part of the Middle Ages. The Musical Instrument Collection of Leipzig University has possibly the oldest dated clavichord that is still preserved [figure 11]. It was made in 1543 by Domenico da Pesaro by whom there is also a fine, well-maintained harpsichord in the same collection.

The small POSITIVE ORGAN was very popular during Renaissance times. As the name (derived from Latin positivum = 'suitable for placing or setting down') implies, this is a small, portable instrument which generally only has one manual, and no pedals or labial pipes. The positive was used in the chancel of the church as a 'choir organ', i.e., to accompany and support the singers and band-players, while the main organ in the nave was kept for solo purposes. The positive was also in great demand as a chamber organ, there being, as yet, no exclusive identification of organ music with places of worship. Many sets of dances, for instance, were written for the positive. Only since the Romantic age has the organ become primarily a church instrument.

One of the few surviving Italian Renaissance positive organs is in the Leipzig University Collection already mentioned [figure 6]. The organ has three ranks of open pipes: four-foot, two-foot and one-foot. (This method of identifying octave pitch, also used for plucked string instruments, derives from the fact

that an eight-foot open pipe length is needed to produce *C* on an organ. A four-foot pipe length gives *c*, i.e., an octave higher, and two-foot gives *ć* ['Middle C'], two octaves higher.) At the back of the instrument there are two wedge-shaped bellows for supplying the necessary wind. On large instruments only trained 'blowers' could be employed, and for special occasions these sometimes had to be hired from abroad. The Leipzig instrument is of strikingly noble proportions. In the true Italian tradition the ends of its keys are decorated with an arcade pattern, the same design that tops the three large arches on the face of the instrument. The stand for the organ also has arcaded decoration.

The social status of music at the time is well expressed in Court Baldassare Castiglione's *Il Cortegiano* in which singing is allowed as a permitted aristocratic accomplishment for the perfect gentleman: 'Harmonious too are all keyed instruments; and with ease many things can be performed on them which fill the soul with the sweetness of music.' This attitude was, of course, later adopted in middle-class families where the girls would be encouraged to take piano lessons but not allowed to study anything as 'vulgar' as the clarinet or drums!

Particularly respectable, in Castiglione's eyes, was solo singing to the accompaniment of a bowed string instrument:

For fine music, replied Messer Federico, group-singing is admirable . . . but still more so is singing to the viola; because the whole sweetness seems to be of one piece; it is possible to follow with far greater attention the beauty of the performance and the aria because the ears only have to concentrate on one part. . . . Most gratifying of all, though, is recitative sung to the viola, which endows the words with almost miraculous charm and efficacy.

This anticipated Baroque monody, but was not entirely new. There had always been instrumentally-accompanied singing — with the minnesingers and trouvères in Europe, as well as elsewhere and earlier.

The 'viola' mentioned here is not the modern instrument of the same name, but this was the generic term for any bowed string instrument. In the present context, for accompanying a solo singer, the instrument intended is almost certainly the LIRA DA BRACCIO. This has a relatively flat body, a heart-shaped

10 A Renaissance organ as depicted in *Angelicum ac divinum opus musice*, 1508, by the famous Italian music theoretician Franchino Gafori (1451–1522).

11 What is thought to be the world's oldest dated clavichord, made by Domenico da Pesaro in 1543, has its keyboard protruding from the side of the instrument (like the Italian spinets). Other typically Italian features are the Gothic patterns on the key-ends and the decorated ends of the keyboard.

12, 13 Giovanni d'Andrea's magnificent lira da braccio, dated 1511. The fingerboard is decorated with inlay *alla certosina* in ivory, ebony and green-coloured horn, a technique favoured in Upper Italy. The two strings projecting from the side of the instrument were employed as drones to strengthen the tone. The richly carved back *(opposite)* contains a wealth of symbolic associations.

tuning head, with upright pegs, five stopped strings and two open strings off the fingerboard, which latter could either be bowed as a bourdon or plucked. By combining the stopped with the open strings the player had at his disposal a simple sort of polyphony that increased the volume of his performance. We know of several precursors of this approach to instrument-building – the medieval hurdy-gurdy, the positive organ in Van Eycks' Ghent altarpiece (where we can clearly discern a device for fixing the bass keys), and the bagpipe that is used to the present day. The immediate predecessor of the lira da braccio (which, incidentally, has nothing except a similarity of name in common with the classical lyre) is, however, the medieval fiddle. It too was often used for the singer to accompany himself. This could be done with complete freedom since both instruments were held loosely against the chest and not pressed under the chin. In all probability simple melodies were favoured that could be repeated strophically, with improvised accompaniment. Leonardo da Vinci is thought to have been a master of this art too, and it is recorded 'he sang divinely to it' (by which is meant the lira he built for himself in the shape of a horse's head).

The oldest surviving lira da braccio is kept by the Vienna Kunsthistorisches Museum. It is also one of the most attractive specimens of this comparatively rare type of instrument. It comes from the Obizzi family's instrument collection that, until 1870, could be seen at Catajo near Padua. The collection was started by Pio Eneas, grandson of the palace's sixteenth-century builder, Marchese Pio degli Obizzi. A contemporary described the 'small, utterly charming theatre...whose walls are furnished with all sorts of musical instruments and books of music. An organ of cypress wood stands on either side' (Betussi, Padua 1573). In 1559 we hear of a private collection kept by Sabba da Castiglione in his Faenza house:

...and so it is that some adorn their houses, because of the beauty of the musical instruments, with organs, harpsichords, monochords [i.e., clavichords], psalteries, harps, dulcimers, pandoras, mandoras and the like; while others pick lutes, violas, violones, liras, flutes, cornetts, tibias, bagpipes, *chianoni* [?], trombones and the like; this adornment is certainly to be lauded because instruments of this sort greatly delight the ear and are highly relaxing to the spirit...furthermore they please the eye when they are the diligent handwork of such excellent and inventive masters as Lorenzo da Pavia and Bastiano da Verona.

Oral and visual pleasure are closely linked too in the splendidly finished Vienna lira [figures 12, 13]. On the outside of the richly decorated back there is a little ivory label with the Greek inscription (in the humanistic mood of the time): 'Song is doctor to the pains of Man', an obvious reference to the healing powers of music. It is the only instrument we know by Giovanni d'Andrea, another Veronese master, and the label inside says 'Joannes Andree Veronen...vosto (agosto?) 1511'.

13

14 The largest of the original leather cases made for the Catajo recorders holds a family of eight and looks almost like a quiver for arrows.

The introduction to the collection of stories by the Florentine writer Antonfrancesco Grazzini gives us a good picture of music-making in aristocratic circles of the time:

In the generous and wonderful city of Florence, after dinner on the last day of January, a holiday, four of the world's finest young gentlemen gathered in the house of a widow – who was as virtuous and as noble as she was rich – to pass the time and to converse with her brother, who, as far as knowledge and graceful manners were concerned, hardly had any equal in Florence or the whole of Tuscany; because the latter, apart from his other virtues, was a perfect musician and kept a room full of choice song-books and praiseworthy instruments, and all the young men could sing and play, some better, some worse.

In such noble surroundings instruments of the most exquisite quality would be expected. These instruments were not artisans' tools but elegant playthings for dilettanti with practically unlimited time and resources.

The outwardly less attractive, simpler wind instruments were generally excluded. Castiglione tells us that these instruments, 'disdained by Minerva', were not the concern of the courtier. This applied, of course, only to their playing. The use of wind instruments by professional musicians was very frequent in aristocratic circles. The nuptial mass to mark the marriage of Constanzo Sforza with Camilla di Aragona in 1475 was celebrated at Pesaro with *pifari e trombetti* (pipers and trumpeters) in attendance. At the wedding of Cosimo dei Medici (Florence, 1539) the *intermezzi* were filled with music played by transverse flutes, trombones and cornetts. A ceremonial wedding breakfast at the court of Ferrara in 1529 was entertained by a band comprising: *1 flauto grosso, 1 dolzaina, 2 flauti mezzani, 1 cornetto sordo, 5 tromboni, 1 cornetto grosso, 4 flauti d'Alemana &c.*

The sweet-sounding RECORDER *(flauto dolce)* seems to have been widespread in sixteenth-century Italy. More than thirty recorders of all pitches – from the tiny *exilent* to the outsize 'great bass' instrument (standing six feet high) – and all presumably from Venetian workshops – were kept at Catajo. Together they form a unique collection of Renaissance recorders, now all in the Vienna Kunsthistorisches Museum [figure 15]. For several of the instruments in this collection the leather-covered cases (presumably also made in Italy) have been preserved. The largest of them takes eight recorders [figure 14]. Also from Renaissance Venice is the first known manual for playing the recorder [figure 17]. 'Conceived by Sylvestro Ganassi dal Fontego, musician to the illustrious authorities of Venice', it is dedicated to the Doge Andrea Gritti. The humanist inspiration comes through in the very first chapter where it is stated that 'all musical instruments are of less value than the human voice, wherefore we attempt to learn from the latter and imitate it'. Just as the painter imitates Nature with various colours so should the flute-player seek to copy the voice.

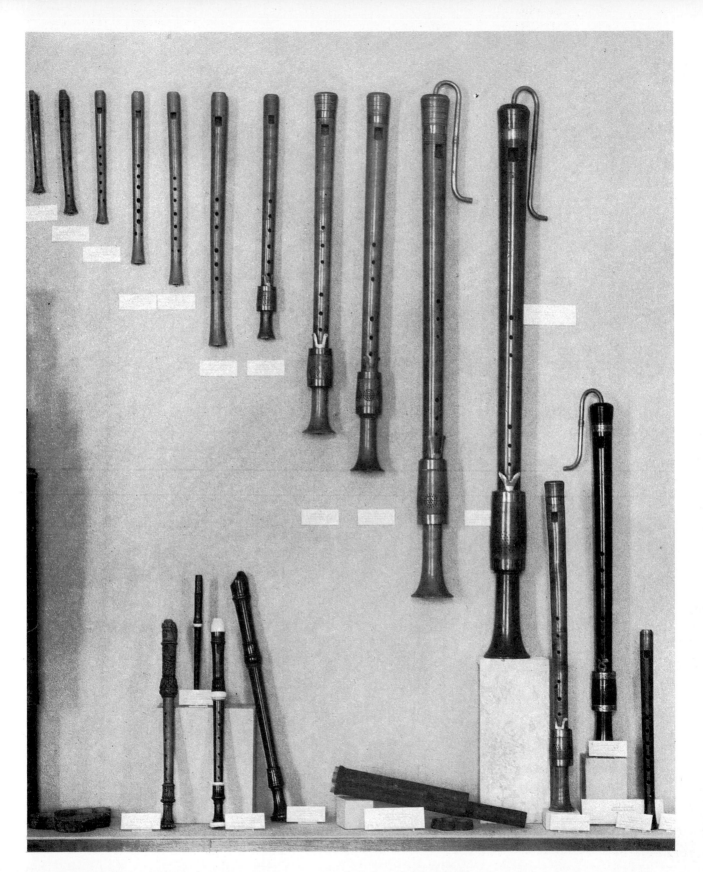

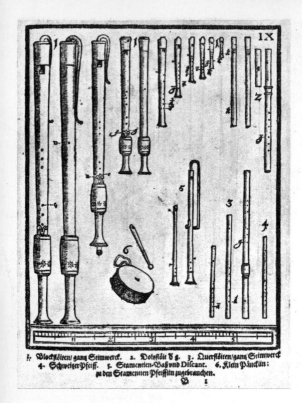

16 Woodcut showing a complete range of recorders.

17 Title-page of the first known recorder manual, Venice, 1535. In the left foreground there is an unopened flute case, in the centre two cornetts, and hanging on the wall a trio of viols and a lute. The instructor (?) on the left is tapping out the rhythm on the player's shoulder.

18 *(opposite)* Cornett- and trombone-players on
16 an Austrian glazed stove-tile, *c.* 1570.

That, as far as social approval of the flute is concerned, other countries took a more indulgent view of this wind instrument is shown by the one-time 'regal' status of the recorder in England. We know that Henry VIII was an accomplished musician and Holinshed tells us that in 1510:

From thense [i.e., from Greenwich] the whole court remooved to Windsor, there beginning his progresse, and exercising himselfe dailie in shooting, singing, dansing, wrestling, casting of the barre, plaieing at the recorders, flute, virginals, in setting of songs, and making of ballads.

Admittedly, flute-playing formed only one aspect of the many courtly distractions of the day, but at Westminster alone the King had no less than seventy-six recorders:

Item one case with vi recorders of Boxe in it
Item viii Recorders greate and smale in a Case couered with blake Leather and lined with clothe
Item twoo base Recorders of waulnuttre, one of them tipped with Siluer: the same are butt redde woode
Item foure Recorders made of okin bowes
Item vi Recorders of Iuerie in a case of blacke vellat
Item one greate base Recorder of woode in a case of woode
Item foure Recorders of waulnuttre in a Case couered with blacke vellat
Item ix Recorders of woode in a Case of woode
Item a case couered with blacke leather with vii recorders all other garnisshements to the same of Siluer gilte with viii recorders of Iuerie in the same Case the twoo bases garnisshed with Siluer and guilte
Item one case of blacke leather with viii recorders of boxe
Item a case of white woode with ix recorders of boxe in the same
Item a case couered with blacke leather with vii recorders of woode in it
Item A litle case couered with blacke leather with iiii recorders of Iuerie in it

In the field of brass instruments particular attention should be paid to the TROMBONE. The first mention of the slide trombone, which is the only version that concerns us here, occurs towards the end of the fifteenth century in the literature of Spain and England (where it is called the sackbut). The instrument probably first appeared in the first half of the fifteenth century having been evolved from the trumpet to which a slide had been fitted. Thanks to the invention of the slide (which enables the player to 'shift' the natural pitch of the instrument and complete the full chromatic scale of overtones) the trombone became one of the most reliable and adaptable wind instruments of the Renaissance. It was used in church music to execute the long-drawn tenor *cantus firmus*-part as well as to play in unison with the singers, but it was also given a part in secular music. The performers were all professionals. Whereas recorders, apparently, came mainly from Venice, Nuremberg was *the* home for brass instruments. Our knowledge of Nuremberg trumpet and trombone makers

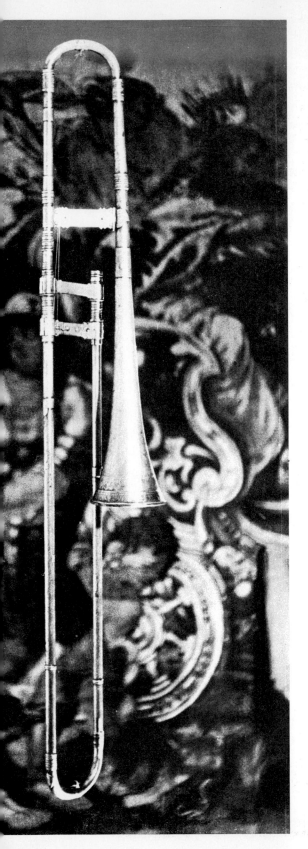

derives especially from the studies published by Fritz Jahn. These artisans all seem to have developed their talents late in the fifteenth century as a special branch of copper-foundry work. In 1479 the city council of Nuremberg granted one Hanns Neuschel his certificate as 'master coppersmith and turner'. He must also have been a good player because in 1499 he was appointed 'trumpeter and piper' to the Nuremberg council. For an annual stipend of fifty-six pounds he undertook to play for the city of Nuremberg at weddings and other events for a period of five years.

One such occasion must have arisen when Emperor Maximilian I was released from imprisonment in Bruges and the council ordered 'the bells of all churches and monasteries to be rung and Te Deums sung, two bonfires to be lit – one on the battlements and one on the market-place – and the town pipers and trumpeters to stand and perform at the portal of the Lady Chapel'. The New Year was also welcomed by the band playing seasonal music from a convenient tower.

We are told that Neuschel's son, also called Hanns, 'carried on his father's handwork after his death'. The younger Neuschel had acquired his certificate as master-craftsman as early as 1493 and pursued his father's trade in exemplary fashion. Since the Nuremberg city council was pleased – presumably for not entirely altruistic reasons – to accept responsibility for all the correspondence with princely courts, the council's records are of tremendous assistance to us in this respect. We find, for instance, that the master, as was then the custom, did not only make trumpets and trombones but also flutes, ivory cornetts, crumhorns, curtals, posthorns, kettle-drums, recorders, pommers and other instruments. Listed among the customers are: Duke Wilhelm of Bavaria (ten trumpets), the Elector of Trier (field trumpets), Duke Friedrich of Schleswig-Holstein, Landgrave Philip of Hesse and even Emperor Maximilian I himself, together with Pope Leo X. As purveyor to Maximilian's court there was never any shortage of work. In 1515 a court trumpeter was sent from Augsburg to Nuremberg to order 'trumpets, clarions and other instruments. . .which are needed for His ride to the King of Hungary and Poland'. Repeatedly Neuschel had to undertake business trips at the Emperor's behest. The pleasure was mixed with anxiety about his wife and children and about the 'noticeable and unfortunate harm' done to his workshop. The extent to which the Emperor valued Neuschel can be judged from the permanent place he was accorded in the 'triumphal procession'. He ordains: 'On one float there shall be five shawms, trombones and crumhorns; and Neuschel shall be in charge with his device carried ahead by a boy: showing how he assembled them to please the Emperor and according to His instructions'.

In 1533 Neuschel died of a current plague and was 'carried to

19 (opposite) This simple, but finely shaped, trombone is of outstanding historical interest. Not only is it the world's second known slide trombone but it is also the only extant instrument made by the Nuremberg master Jörg Neuschel.

burial on two biers with twelve candles'. The son of Hanns Neuschel the Younger, Jörg Neuschel, was the last member of the family to practise the trade. He too had the most illustrious customers, even more illustrious if anything than those of his father before him: Duke Albrecht in Prussia, the King of Denmark, the King of Poland, Margrave Joachim of Brandenburg, the Electors of Saxony, the Electors of the Rhineland, the King of England. He himself was totally convinced of the high standard of his workmanship and said: 'I for my part am satisfied that no one can compare, either in Germany or abroad.' As the Nuremberg councillor Hieronymus Schürstab confirms, his instruments were 'made with great exactitude, cunning and curiosity'. Their prices were accordingly somewhat high, often three or four times that charged for other 'German or foreign instruments'. With Jörg Neuschel's death in 1557 in Nuremberg his workshop closed, and other names came to the fore.

Only one of Neuschel's instruments is known to us, a brass tenor slide trombone, with the inscription *MACHT JORG NEVSCHEL ZV NVRMB. MDLVII* (making it one of his last instruments) around the bell. On the rim is stamped an imperial crown; there is evidence in the Nuremberg archives that this was a privilege accorded to the Neuschels in 1515 [figure 19].

20 This detail from the famous series of woodcuts entitled *Kayser Maximilian I Triumph* shows the Emperor's favourite instrument-maker, Hanns Neuschel, surrounded by shawm, crumhorn and trombone players.

Mannerism

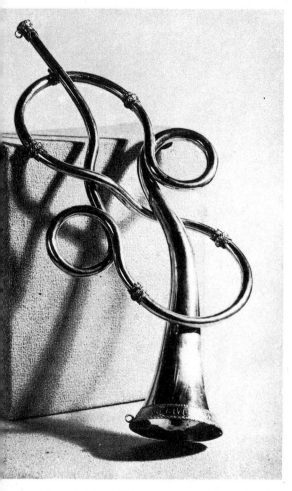

THE NEW STYLE WROUGHT LITTLE CHANGE in musical instruments, and even the occasional Mannerist features had sometimes emerged during the High Renaissance. During the Mannerist period music gained in overall importance. The motionless equilibrium of the Renaissance gave way to dynamic, temporal flow. Both architecture and sculpture were rhythmified and 'musicalized'. Everything was drawn gradually into motion, winding in and out through serpentines and labyrinths. Poetry was transformed into pure dashing verbal music. Paintings gushed forth with streams of glowing colour. Architectural mazes and whirlpools engulfed the observer. What better description could there be than this Eulogy of Orpheus' Song by Cavaliere Marino, the poetic protagonist of Mannerism:

Talhor quasi volubile Meandro	Often like inconstant Meander,
O'Labirinto obliquo	Or confusing labyrinth
Per anguste torture	Through torturous straits
Di flessuosa scala	Of twisting scales
Serpendo in lungo giro	Winding in lengthy turns
S'increspa, e piega, e si rivolge,	It curls, bends, revolves,
[e rota.	[rotates.

Musical forces were now concentrated. Imposing massivity was the ideal. For instance, for the performance of one work by Striggio – at the Munich marriage of Duke Wilhelm v of Bavaria to Renata of Loraine in 1568 – forty executants were specified: eight trombones, eight viols, eight large flutes, a lute, an *instrumento da penna* (harpsichord?), and voices.

Instruments were sometimes decorated at unbelievable expense. The SPINET by one Annibale dei Rossi of Milan is adorned with 1,928 precious and semi-precious stones and must accordingly be ranked among the world's (materially) most valuable instruments, since the jewels include turquoise, lapis lazuli, topaz, emerald, sapphire, garnet, pearl, amethyst, jasper, cornelian and ruby. Paolo Morigia was probably referring to this instrument when he wrote in 1595:

This skilful maker constructed among other works a clavichord [the then accepted name for any keyboard instrument] of uncommon beauty and excellence, with the keys all of precious stones and with the most elegant ornaments. This instrument was sold for five hundred crowns, and is now in the possession of the learned and refined nobleman Signor Carlo Trivulzio.

22 This labyrinthine trumpet is clearly of the Mannerist period. Its intricately woven tube is almost terrifyingly, dynamically alive. The bronze-gilt instrument has decorated silver knobs, and is marked in silver lettering *MACHT ANTONI SCHNITZER IN NVRMBERG MDXXXVII.*

21 *(opposite)* Detail of a spinet by Giovanni Celestini [figure 26], Venice, 1589. The jack-rail and the border around the top of the instrument have the ivory buttons commonly found in Italy. The fine rosette, of thin veneer and embossed parchment, is in elaborate Gothic style.

The spinet, signed *ANNIBALIS DE ROXIS MEDIOLANENSES MDLXXVII*, is now the property of the Victoria and Albert Museum in London [figures 25, 29].

Another of the Museum's spinets, one said to have been owned by Queen Elizabeth of Bohemia, also has exceptionally voluptuous decoration. The case is covered with leather mounted with mythological scenes made from enamel and coloured Murano glass [figure 32]. Italian spinet-makers were altogether in great demand at the time. Many of their instruments were still in use centuries later. There is a portrait of the young Mozart, for instance, (painted 1770 in Verona by Saverio dalla Rosa) showing the boy at a spinet made by Giovanni Celestini of Venice and dated 1583 [figure 23]. Seven instruments by Celestini (documented between 1583 and 1610) have been preserved to our day. Two of them are in Vienna – one in the Kunsthistorisches Museum, the other in the author's collection. The second of these was made in 1589. It has a rich rosette (in Gothic style!) made of parchment and thin veneer. Its body, decorated with ivory buttons, is firmly fixed in a simple, solid housing, the outside of which is painted in a uniform dark green. Inside the cover there are paintings which may be of somewhat later origin but are still clearly of the Mannerist period [figures 21, 24, 26].

By the second half of the sixteenth century Flemish instrument-makers were in the ascendant. For generations the Ruckers family of Antwerp held undisputed sway. Handel himself owned a Ruckers harpsichord. The first member of the dynasty was Hans Ruckers the Elder who was admitted to the

23 Mozart in boyhood sitting at a spinet made by Giovanni Celestini; painting by Saverio dalla Rosa, 1770. The maker is clearly identified on the front panel by the words *IOANNIS CELESTINI VENETI MDLXXXIII*.

24 The keys with their ivory buttons and the board bearing the maker's name *IOANNIS CELESTINI VENETI MDLXXXIX* of the Celestini spinet, [figure 26], Venice, 1589. The late Gothic patterns at the front end of the keys are clearly visible.

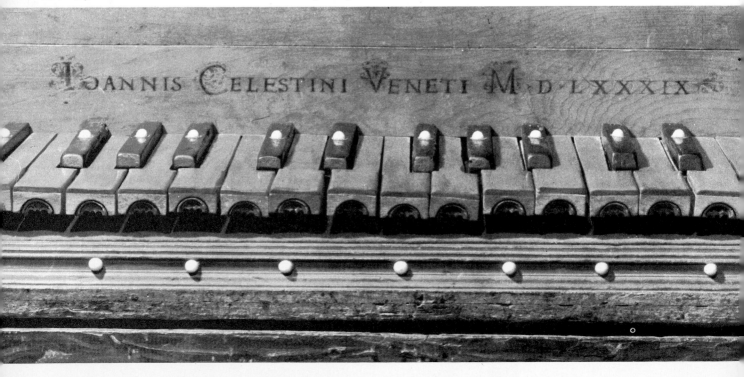

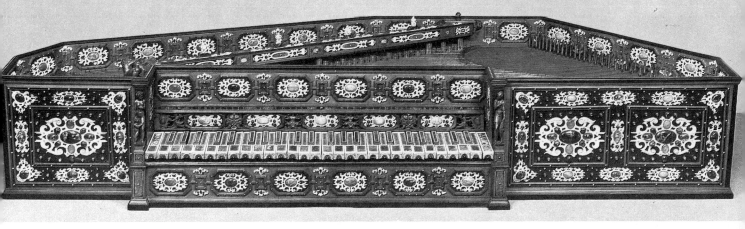

25 Annibale dei Rossi's spinet set with ivory and precious and semi-precious stones.

Guild of St Luke in 1575 as 'clavisinbalmakerre'. The family tradition of craftsmanship was a recognized feature of the age. Parallel instances can be found in painting (the Bassano, Brueghel, Cranach families) and in other fields.

The Flemish VIRGINAL (the disputed origin of whose name may be *virga* = rod, jack) has its strings running parallel to the fingerboard or at a slight angle to it. Like the Italian spinet it too has only one stop. In the Low Countries the comparatively high case tends to be rectangular in shape, with the keyboard recessed into it. The lower ('white') keys are generally of bone and without the usual Italian decorative pattern. The usual pinewood case is often decorated with patterned paper. The cast-lead rosette which incorporates the maker's initials later had bronze paint applied to it. The maker's sign was not – as in Italy – on the panel

26 Spinet by Giovanni Celestini, Venice, 1589. It is the second oldest surviving instrument by Celestini, who was one of Italy's leading harpsichord-makers. In the middle of the painted lid Venus and Cupid are seen asleep attended by *putti*. In the left panel a *putto* in herald's costume blows a trumpet, and on the right a monkey is busy leafing through some sheets of music. The arches on either side are supported by caryatids. The bizarre base – with marine monsters, shells, etc. – is of later date (Venice, *c*. 1700) than the instrument itself.

23

27 Hexagonal Italian spinet in its exterior case. The instrument, which bears the arms of Elizabeth I, was almost certainly in the Queen's possession. It is clear that even in England the virginal never entirely supplanted the Italian spinet.

28 The title-page of *Parthenia*, the first collection of engraved music for keyboard instruments, London, 1611, with compositions by William Byrd, John Bull and Orlando Gibbons. There are many pictures from the seventeenth century which show that the virginal was a popular instrument with the fair sex.

PARTHENIA

or

THE MAYDENHEAD

of the first musicke that

euer was printed for the VIRGINALLS.

COMPOSED

By three famous Masters: William Byrd. D: John Bull, & Orlando Gibbons
Gentlemen of his Maᵗⁱᵉˢ most Illustrious Chappell.
Dedicated to all the Maisters and Louers of Musick.

Ingrauen

by (William Hole)

for

DOROTHIE EVANS

Cum

Priuilegio.

Printed at LONDON by G. Lowe and ... are to be fould

over the keyboard but generally on the jack-rail (whose purpose is to check the jacks from springing out – 'like the reins of a horse' as one sixteenth-century description puts it). Just as in Italy, though, the case is rested on a table or stand. The sound-board is painted with fruit and flower designs. The inside of the cover is also usually decorated with pictures of contemporary society (rather than with mythological subjects). The courtly world of the cavalier and his lady at pleasure in park or garden is a favourite theme. Room is often found too for an uplifting motto such as: *SIC TRANSIT GLORIA MVNDI, MVSICA DVLCE LABORVM LEV AMEN, MVSICA DONVM DEI, MVSICA MAGNORVM EST SOLAMEN DVLCE LABORVM,* or *OMNIS SPIRITVS LAVDET DOMINVM IN CORDIS ET ORGANO LAVDATE EVM IN CYMBALIS BENE SONANTIBVS.* Musical instruments of this sort thus symbolize the conception of a *Gesamtkunstwerk,* so pupular at the time, in that they combine sound, shape, colour and guiding thought.

The Boston Museum of Fine Arts has an attractive virginal (dated 1610) made by Andreas Ruckers the Elder (born 1579 in Antwerp). Andreas Ruckers was the son of Hans Ruckers the Elder, the founder of the dynasty. The jack-rail is marked on top *ANDREAS RVCKERS ME FECIT ANTVERPIA* [figure 30].

The virginal seems to have been greatly appreciated in England where the name was popularly derived from the Latin *virgo* = maiden, with specific reference to Elizabeth, the 'virgin queen'. In *Memoirs of my own Life,* 1564, Sir James Melville, the Scottish diplomat, wrote: 'Then sche [Elizabeth] asked wither the Queen [Mary, of the Scots] or sche played best. In that I gaif hir the prayse.' However a terminological complication arises in that the word 'virginal' was sometimes also used in reference to the Italian spinet and the harpsichord.

One of Queen Elizabeth's instruments is today preserved in the Victoria and Albert Museum. Its cypress-wood case is covered with 'crimson Genoa velvet' and lined with 'yellow tabby silk'. The keys are adorned with gold, silver and ivory inlay-work. The Queen's arms are displayed in both sides [figure 27].

29 Detail of a spinet by Annibale dei Rossi [figure 25], Milan, 1577, one of the choicest keyboard instruments ever made. The decoration is of ivory set with precious and semi-precious stones, and the keys themselves have rich and elaborate inlay with costly applications.

Among the strange keyboard instruments of the time were the GLÖGGLEN-WERKE, bell devices described as 'domestic instruments for playing spiritual airs'. The little bells in tuned series were made of metal, china or glass and were struck by hammers activated through keys. These perhaps originated as imitations of the carillons that were so popular in the Netherlands.

The 1593 Musical Instrument Inventory of the Dresden Electorate lists 'an instrument with little bells, not all of whose

Immense fourteen-pointed cymbal-star of late-Gothic, pseudo-oriental pattern with a large number of small bells attached. This is a reminder of the ancient magical connotation of sound as reflected to the present day in the acolyte's bells rung during the Roman Catholic mass. This cymbal-star was admired by all who saw and heard it during the seventeenth century in the church of Fulda, Germany. Illustration from Athanasius Kircher's *Musurgia Universalis*, Rome, 1650.

keys function'. Curt Sachs published the travel notes of one Philipp Hainhofer who, in 1617, spent some time at the Court of Berlin. He describes how Prince Joachim Siegismund (then fourteen years old) took him by the hand and showed him a '*Glögglen-Werk* suitable for performing the Psalms'. The same term is found in several organs for a manual stop and sometimes for the pedal. In this case the 'bells' are usually metal bars.

Austria's remarkable Art and Curiosity Chamber of Ambras Castle (near Innsbruck) once had a 'bell-piano', now in the Vienna Kunsthistorisches Museum, which was listed as 'an instrument with glass devices'. It was probably made in Tirol in the second half of the sixteenth century. The actual bells – still noted in the 1821 Ambras inventory – are all missing. Inside the wooden case there is only the playing mechanism. Felt-covered hammers are thrown up by keys. The keyboard, presumably ranging from *C–a"*, protrudes from the cabinet in the Italian fashion. The front of the keys displays the typical Italian arcade pattern. Above the keys, between Mars and Minerva (sym-

30 This virginal in the usual rectangular box shape was made in 1610 by Andreas Ruckers the Elder, one of the earliest members of a famous family of plucked-string keyboard instrument-makers. Ruckers instruments once enjoyed the same sort of fame now accorded to violins by Stradivari or Guarneri.

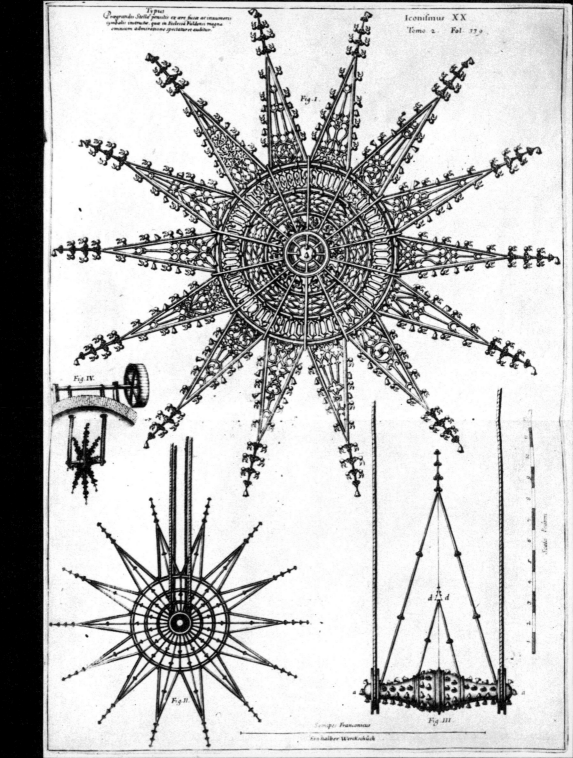

Typus

Praegrandis Stellae penulti ex aere fusae ac innumeris symbolis instructae, quae in Ecclesia Fuldensi magna omnium admiratione spectatur et auditur.

Fig. I.

Fig. IV.

Fig. II.

Fig. III.

Scala Pedum

d   d

a   a

Semipes Franconicus

Ein halber Werckschuch.

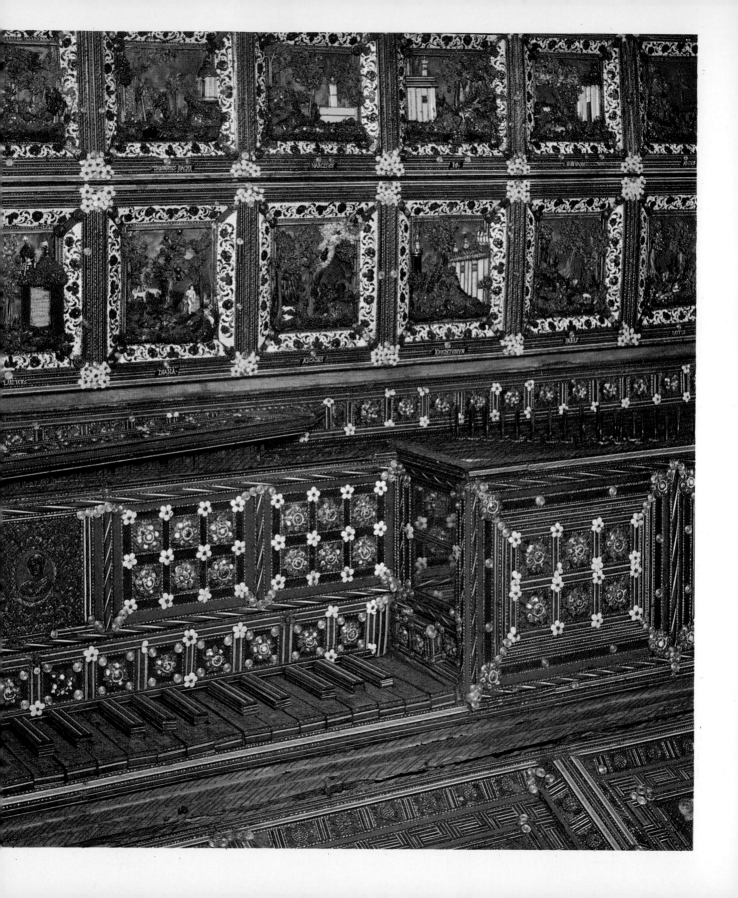

33 Italian octave spinet, *c.* 1600, with a painted
lid showing the mythological musician Arion
rescued by a dolphin and charming the inhabitants
of the seas.

32 *(opposite)* Detail of late sixteenth-century
Italian spinet [figure 25]. Lavish decorations of
enamel and Murano glass adorn the instrument
and the leather-covered case. The ornamental
panels show scenes from classical mythology.

bolizing War and Art), there are the arms of Archduke Ferdinand
of Tirol for whom the instrument was made [figure 35].

Ambras Castle was the original home of several particularly
valuable instruments in the Vienna collection. Situated on a
hillside overlooking the Tirolean capital, Ambras was the
favourite residence of Archduke Ferdinand. We have a colourful
description of it given in 1574 by Stephanus Venandus Pighius.
In his *Hercules prodicius* he calls Ambras 'a castle like a palace,
a magnificent villa of very graceful appearance and in the most
beautiful position, with pictures and princely chattels'. He then
proceeds to admire 'the graceful furnishings, courtyards, halls
and refectories decorated with carpets, statues, paintings'. The
surroundings of the castle are equally pleasurable: 'In the
exquisitely tended gardens there are paradises, labyrinths and

29

34 Archduke Ferdinand of Austria (1529–95).

35 Bell-piano from Ambras Castle in Tirol. The entire instrument is painted in oils on white ground, probably by Dionys of Hallert, the Flemish artist who was employed at Ambras in decorating the Spanish Hall.

grottoes dedicated to water-nymphs and watered from artificial springs.' There then follows an account of the diversions that were a feature of the age. They include 'a round table under which there are water-driven wheels which turn the table together with those seated at it in slow or quick tempo thus making the people dizzy'. For the chronicler this is then followed by a visit to 'a sanctuary of the wine-god... a mighty dark, rocky cave'. In a world of this sort which was constantly seeking *maraviglia* great stress was naturally laid on collecting curious musical instruments.

The Ambras Instrument Chamber, which formed the basis for the present Vienna Collection of Old Music Instruments, contained some of the most curious and costly instruments that we know today. However, the instruments constituted only one section of the original Ambras miscellany. Following the death of his dearly loved spouse, Philippine Welser, Ferdinand turned practically his whole castle into a museum, with a valuable library, a coin cabinet, an array of arms and armour, a selection of portrait and paintings, a collection of all sorts of 'rare and monstrous animals, antlers and bones', a gallery of classical antiquities, a collection of sculptures, a vast selection of the most varied types of items of applied art made of horn, wood, ivory, pottery, wax, *papier mâché*, enamel, mother-of-pearl, etc., precious *objets d'art* of gold and silver, glass-paintings and intricate glass objects, clocks, mathematical instruments, unique mechanical toys, curios from Turkey, India and China, silver beakers, rock-crystal vases, carved stones, manuscripts, engravings and so on. All the musical instruments were kept in the fourth, so-called 'white' cabinet in the lower wing of the castle. The 1596 inventory includes, for example:

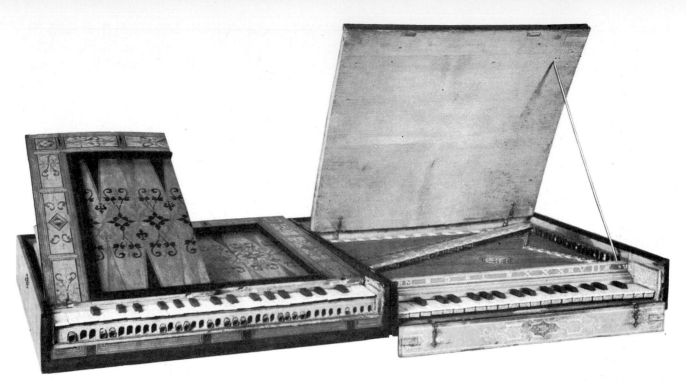

36 A combination of spinet, regal and games case, from the Ambras collection. On the left is a regal with its two-part bellows, and on the right an octave spinet. On the jack-rail is inscribed in white letters *SIC TRANSIT GLORIA MVNDI*. The board over the keys is marked *MDLXXXVII* and at the back there is the inscription *ANTHONIVS MEIDLING AVGVSTANVS FECIT ANNO DOM. 1587 MENSAE DECEMBRIJ.*

(following spread)
37 Allegory of Love, or Spring; Flemish painting, *c.* 1600. Love, represented as a young lutenist, is seated in a spring landscape. At his feet are various pieces of equipment for sports and games, books devoted to the art of love, three part-books and a number of musical instruments: on the left, a four-stringed fretted viol with turned-back peg-box and a bow, and a black curved cornett; on the right a cittern, a leather flute case, and a richly lined leather case for his lute.

An instrument combining regal and positive with Frog-croak, Birdsong and many other stops
An instrument looking like a board game containing a regal and its appurtenances
In a case, five *'tardöld'* shaped like dragons
One large strange lute with two necks and three stars
One trumpet all in silver with gilt trimmings
One cittern with Lucretia Romano carved on its neck

– all of whose appearance is in some way exceptional.

In another of his castles, Ruhelust, the Archduke kept instruments of more practical use, as the same inventory shows. Here are listed some two hundred and fifty trumpets, kettledrums, trombones, flutes, viols, liras, lutes, bagpipes, clavichords, dulcians, shawms and the like.

The 'instrument looking like a board game' actually comprised two keyboard instruments, SPINET and REGAL. (Combinations of this sort – which were given names like *claviorgana* – were not unknown at the time. Their production seems to have centred around the cities of Nuremberg and Augsburg.) The two-part case, when closed, can be used for chess and draughts, and opens up to display a backgammon board [figure 36]. This is, of course, a classical combination which we still find now, centuries later. In the left-hand half there is a small regal with wind supplied by bellows; the spinet is on the right. The regal is a miniature organ with reed pipes only, giving it a nasal, growling tone quality. Its middle- and bass-notes 'speak' quite nicely. The higher notes are a more tricky proposition and need frequent retuning. (Praetorius noticed the same drawback in the 'bible-regal' which he made in

VER

33

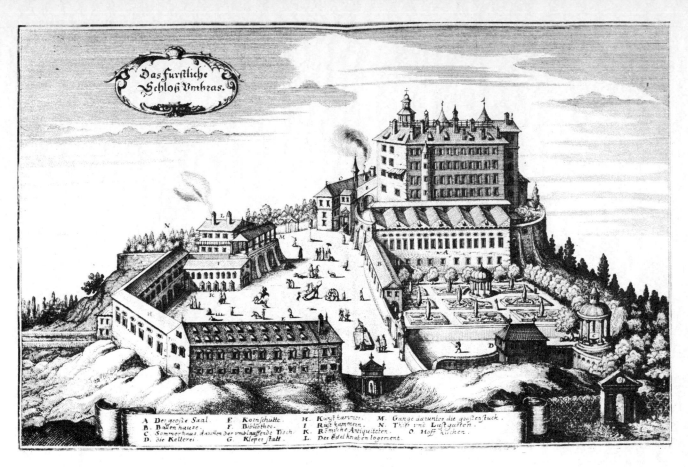

Das fürstliche Schloß Umbras.

A. Der große Saal.   E. Kornschutte.   H. Kunstkammer.   M. Gange darunter die großen Stuck.
B. Ballenhause.   F. Bibliothec.   I. Rustkammen.   N. Thür und Lustgarten.
C. Sommerhaus darinnen der umblauffende Tisch. K. Römische Antiquitäten. O. Hoff Kirchen.
D. die Kellerei.   G. Klepper stall.   L. Der Edelknaben logement.

39 Engraving of Ambras Castle in Tirol, the favourite residence of Archduke Ferdinand, which stands on a hill on the outskirts of Innsbruck. The extensive complex of buildings contains cellars, granaries, a tennis court, a library, armouries, Roman antiquities, and lodgings for the boys of the household, as well as a menagerie and a hunting ground.
In the right foreground the summer-house (C) can be seen, a small pavilion in which stands the 'turning table'. The art-gallery (H) in the left foreground was where the collection of musical instruments was housed.

38 (opposite) Double-manual regal in Kremsmünster Abbey showing the two ranks of wooden pipes behind which is a series of labial metal pipes. At each end of the upper manual there are three stops. The buttons underneath the male and female fauns are for joke-stops. The instrument belonged to an abbot of Garsten who brought it to Kremsmünster with his own private organist.

Nuremberg.) The spinet is, strictly speaking, an octave spinet, since it sounds an octave higher than the normal instrument.

Mention should be made at this point of a positive organ built in south Germany towards the end of the sixteenth-century. It is unusual in that it combines reed pipes and labial pipes, and also has two manuals. The organ has two 'faces'. The back one displays the labial metal pipes; the front one, where the keyboard is, has the reed pipes. At each end of the intarsio keyboard there is a carved, painted figure. To the left is a horned male, to the right a female faun. Buttons near the figures can be pushed in to operate the fanciful stops: Trumpet-Drone or Bagpipe-Quint on the left, a fluty Cuckoo Call on the right. There are signs that the figures once held movable instruments (presumably a shepherd's horn and a flute) [figure 38]. 'Joke stops' were quite common in those days. They included all sorts of cymbals and bells, Birdsong, Foxtail (described as 'difficult to push back if anyone has the temerity to pull it out'), Side-Drum, Kettle-Drum, Eagle, Sun, Nightingale, Tamborine, etc. In later days the first pianofortes upheld this tradition. Mozart's *Rondo alla turca* is written for a piano with built-in Drum and Cymbal stops.

Quite the most exquisite instrument in the Ambras collection was the CITTERN specially made for Archduke Ferdinand by

40 *(left)* Cittern of stained and carved
maple wood made in Urbino in 1582.

41 *(right)* The richly ornamented peg-box
of the cittern made by Girolamo de Virchis for
Archduke Ferdinand of Tirol [figure 42]. Lucretia,
who is emerging from a dragon's mouth, elegantly
thrusts a dagger into her bosom from which
blood is beginning to stream. The back of the
neck is formed by a naked woman, a lizard-like
animal and a grotesque face. This wild jumble of
horrific, ugly and beautiful features is
characteristic of the Mannerist age.

43 *(right)* Constructional diagram (*c.* 1435) of a
lute, an instrument of Middle Eastern origin
whose pear shape is of timeless perfection.

42 Archduke Ferdinand's cittern.

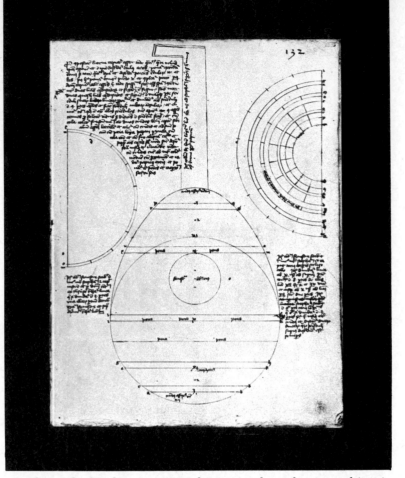

Girolamo de Virchis, a *citeraro* known to have been working in
Brescia between 1563 and 1568 and to have been in close contact
with the famous *luthier* Gasparo da Salò. The Ambras cittern is
the master's only extant instrument. The cittern, a widely
popular plucked instrument in the sixteenth, seventeenth and
eighteenth centuries, has a characteristically pear-shaped body
with flat belly and back, double-course wire strings, and frets,
and is usually played with the fingers. In the present case the
exceptionally opulent finish given to the instrument can
probably be accounted for by the importance of the personage
by whom it had been ordered. The ribs and back of choicest
palisander are protected by brilliant amber varnish and adorned
with a wealth of ornaments. The top of the peg-box is in the
form of a carved torso of Lucretia emerging from a dragon's
throat. The carefully coifed lady – wearing a necklace and
earrings, but not much else – is on the point of thrusting a dagger
into her bosom from which a trickle of highly naturalistic blood
is already beginning to flow. The back of the peg-box has
another naked woman above a grotesque face whose hook-like

nose can be used by the player to hold the instrument. At the place where the fingerboard covers the belly a girl stands far from coyly in the mouth of a cornucopia. The rosette too is a mass of intricate ornament and delicate colouring, among which we can pick out two *putti*, one winged *putto*-head, four sphinxes, two face masks, and the red eagle of Tirol. The heel of the inlaid back incorporates Ferdinand's coat of arms, above which there are two female busts holding the archducal cap [figures 41, 42].

The MANDORA can best be described as a small-sized lute. Unlike the lute, though, with its characteristic sharp bend at the top of the neck, the mandora's peg-box just tails off approximately in the same plane. There are generally four courses of strings. A mandora in the Victoria and Albert Museum, made in the latter half of the sixteenth century, comes from France, a country where, according to Praetorius in 1618, the instrument was especially popular. Like the medieval rebec it is constructed on a very old principle, the body being carved out of a single block of wood, and not built up of ribs like a lute [figure 44].

The LUTE derives, in both name and shape, from the Arab *al'ud*. It was brought to Europe by the Moors and Saracens and became one of the most popular instruments from the fifteenth to the seventeenth century [figure 43]. The pear-shaped back of its body is formed of a number of flat ribs. The flat belly has a sound-hole whose rosette is usually intricately carved. The pear shape is of supreme classical beauty, and major modifications of it are structurally impossible. It is also out of the question to find room for any carving or other added ornament on this delicately built instrument. The only alternative, sometimes practised, was to choose costly materials for its construction. There are, for instance, lutes made of strips of ivory or even tortoiseshell, such as the Burkholtzer instrument in the Vienna Kunsthistorisches Museum [figure 46].

We find countless reports of painters who played the lute and this can perhaps be accounted for in part by the instrument's purely visual beauty – but only in part. Vasari, for instance, tells us of Giorgione that 'he was particularly fond of the sound of the lute, and in his time he played it so divinely that he was frequently called upon to perform at musical gatherings'. Sebastiano del Piombo seems to have spent more time playing than working at his easel so that 'many report Sebastiano's chief occupation was not painting but music; because in addition to singing he delighted in performing on various instruments, above all the lute'.

44 The back of this French mandora, dating from the later part of the sixteenth century, is completely covered with ornaments in relief. The three naked woman in the middle can be identified as Juno, Diana, and Venus accompanied by Cupid, and behind the peg-box is Medusa's head.

One of the most famous families of bowed- and plucked-string instrument-makers, the Tieffenbruckers, was probably of Bavarian origin but all its members worked abroad: Wendelin Tieffenbrucker in Padua (from 1551 to 1611); Magno Tieffenbrucker – probably two generations of the same name – in Venice (from 1557 to 1621); and Kaspar Tieffenbrucker – otherwise known as Gaspard Duiffoprugcar – in Lyons (where he died in 1570). One of the choicest works of the *luthier*'s art is the VIOLA DA GAMBA that Kaspar made for François I.

The gamba is a six-stringed bowed instrument whose waisted shape tapers off towards the top to a point. Its ribs are comparatively deep, the belly arched, the back flat, and it has frets. It first appeared as a bass instrument and only later did it come to be made in a smaller sizes. The 'viols as large as myself', seen by Bernardo Prospero in 1493 in Mantua, were certainly gambas.

François I's instrument *'au plan de la ville de Paris'* is remark-

45   Allegory of the moon by Hendrik Goltzius (1558–1617). Luna, depicted as Diana with bows and hunting dogs, is tweaking the leg of a lute-playing cavalier next to her. The gentle moonlit landscape is a mass of fountains and loving couples. The moon has always been associated with water – especially the ebb and flood of the tides, as well as night-time moisture – and love.

able for its elaborate marquetry work, in particular for its bird's-eye view of the city on the back made of different inlaid woods [figures 47, 48]. It is a truly kingly instrument, ideally suited for the *roi-chevalier*, master of all the arts of love and war, himself a brilliant raconteur and poet, who summoned numerous Italian Mannerist artists, among them Benvenuto Cellini, to Paris.

The Gemeentemuseum in The Hague has a somewhat simpler gamba by Kaspar Tieffenbrucker [figure 50] whose fingerboard displays the delightful maxim:

VIVA FVI IN SILVIS SVM DVRA OCCISA SECVRI
DVM VIXI TACVI MORTVA DVLCE CANO

(I was alive in the woods: I was cut down by the cruel axe. While I lived I was silent: In death I sweetly sing.)

46 *(below left)* Lute whose body is constructed of twenty-one ivory ribs. The handwritten label inside says *Hanns Burkholtzer, Lautern/macher in Fiessen 1596.*

47, 48 *(below centre and right)* The *viole au plan de la ville de Paris* made for François I. Its soundboard is strewn with marquetry representations of dragonflies, flowers, birds and *chinoiseries*. The back has a bird's-eye view of Paris and, above it, St Luke with his bull sitting on a cloud. The peg-box is shaped like an animal in the front and a human face at the back.

49 Column flute, late sixteenth century. So as not to upset the architectural symmetry with a mouthpiece, the instrument is blown through a hole hidden beneath the capital behind a decorated metal flap.

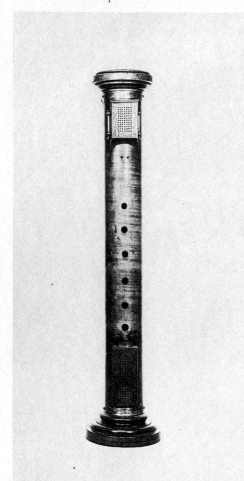

– a moving reminder that instruments can bring dead animal and plant material to life again.

Most unusual are the COLUMN FLUTES found in Brussels and Paris. These offer just one of many possible examples of the way in which Mannerist architectural principles were applied to other art forms. All sorts of furniture, caskets and everyday objects – as well as musical instruments – had architectural pretensions, and the surprise effect caused by this unsuitable choice of medium was assured [figure 49].

Another organological curiosity from the Ambras collection is the type of RACKET it contains. The purpose of this instrument was to compress the necessary length for a bass instrument of the double-blade reed type into the smallest possible space. For this the bores are 'squeezed' into a thick cylinder like a string of sausages when bundled together. The two ivory rackets at Ambras [figure 51] are itemized in the 1596 inventory as '*zwei helfenbaine gleiche tartaldi*', thus relating them to the *tardöld* instruments already mentioned which are of the shawn type but also have a twisted tube inside their dragon bodies. The cylinder was bored in such a way that the total effective pipe-length is more than nine times that of the block itself. The many twists and turns account for its lack of volume and, as Praetorius said, 'the resonance is rather muffled so that it sounds like blowing through a comb'. All the same these instruments can go almost as low as a double bass without being higher than the width of a hand. The Ambras rackets, for instance, measure just $4\frac{3}{4}$ inches! Since everyone 'knows' that deep notes correspond to large dimensions and vice versa – whether in string length, tube bore, organ pipe size or the body dimensions of plucked or bowed instruments – their obvious incongruity gives them a clear qualification for inclusion in any collection of curiosities. Who has ever heard of a dwarf with a *basso profundo* voice? Nevertheless rackets really were used by musicians [figure 54] and can be seen today in many museums, although they are mostly made of less precious wood.

An instrument frequently encountered during the Mannerist period was the CORNETT. Made of wood or ivory this is a cross between a woodwind and a brass instrument – although it has fingerholes it is played with a cupped mouth-piece. Because of its penetrating sound it provided a welcome substitute for the trumpet, whose players were strictly organized in guilds. All the same it was capable of being performed with great subtlety and even virtuosity. When monody began to break through in the instrumental field the cornett was immediately to the fore. We frequently find the indication 'for solo violin or cornett'. Instrumentation in its modern sense as yet meant nothing, and the widely varying tonal qualities of violin and cornett were considered interchangeable. Much more important at the time

51 Two ivory descant rackets from Ambras.
The nine interconnected pipes in the body of
each instrument make the fingering very
complicated, some fingers having to cover
several holes at once.

50 Viola da gamba by Kaspar Tieffenbrucker
with a strange, unusually slim body.

was the technical aspect. Provided compass, playability and
dynamic scale were comparable then the actual choice of
instrument was of secondary relevance.

As far as cornetts were concerned there were two types, the
curved and the straight (or mute) cornetts. The curved cornett,
fashioned in an eight-sided shape, was put together from two
separate halves, generally of wood (such as maple, box, plum or
walnut) and covered with leather, or of costly ivory [figure 53].
The centre for cornett manufacture seems to have been Venice
where – according to Vincenzo Galilei in his *Dialogo* (1581) – 'the
best present-day ones are made'. Nuremberg had a famous
maker too, one Neuschel who sold 'ivory cornetts' to Duke
Albrecht in Prussia. One of the most prominent performers –
against his will – was Benvenuto Cellini. In his autobiography
he describes without any attempt at modesty how skilled he was
at playing the cornett. It all began with his father, he tells us,
who 'at that time built wonderful organs with wooden pipes,
the finest harpsichords that could be seen, viols, lutes and the
most excellent harps' in addition to being one of the Medici

43

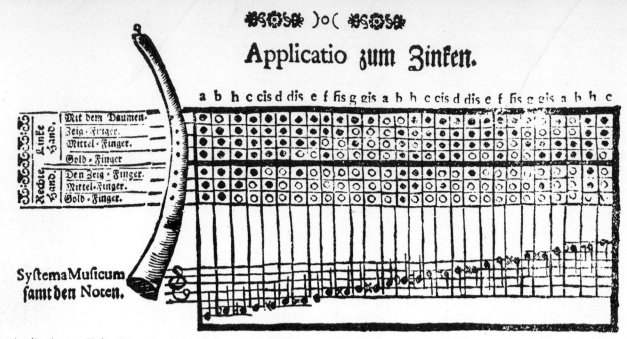

a b h c cis d dis e f fis g gis a b h c cis d dis e f fis g gis a b h c

| Linke Hand | Mit dem Daumen. |
| Zeig-Finger. |
| Mittel-Finger. |
| Gold-Finger. |
| Rechte Hand | Den Zeig-Finger. |
| Mittel-Finger. |
| Gold-Finger. |

Syſtema Muſicum ſamt den Noten.

52 *Applicatio zum Zinken* (Fingering Table for Cornett) in Casper Majer's *Museum Musicum*, 1732. Since the cornett was not restricted to guild use it was a popular instrument in the eighteenth century for town-musicians, and was occasionally scored for by Johann Sebastian Bach in his compositions.

53 Two curved cornetts. The famous French theoretician Mersenne wrote enthusiastically about the sound of this instrument (which died out in the nineteenth century): 'When heard among voices singing in church or chapel, it is like a ray of sunlight brightening the shadows.'

54 *(opposite)* Ivory carving (1618–24) by the Munich court artist Christof Angermaier. Pan, the shepherd's god, takes part in a pastoral concert. On the left in the foreground are a curved cornett, racket and bass recorder (in column shape); on the right a trombone and descant pommer. Visible in the background are flute, pommer and crumhorn.

'pipers'. Cellini senior was evidently determined that his obviously gifted son should likewise become a musician. Benvenuto was less than keen on 'accursed music-making' but nevertheless assisted in motet performances for the Pope, playing the treble part on a cornett. But Cellini did not let 'the most wanton cornett' keep him from his beloved *orificeria*, the goldsmith's art.

There can be no doubt, though, that a perfectly played cornett must have had an enchanting effect. In his *Delle imperfetioni della musica moderna*, an attack on the current monodic style, Aretusi stresses that 'the cornett is capable of imitating the human voice'.

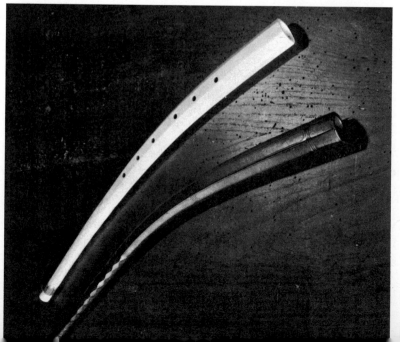

High Baroque

THE TREND TOWARDS INDIVIDUALISM which first became apparent in Mannerist music – with a leading voice on top, a separate bass line at the bottom, and an accompaniment filling the gap in the middle – now became firmly established. It was the musical equivalent, in a way, of the supremacy Machiavelli accorded his *Prince*. The idea of polyphonic equality was replaced with a solo part supported by a strong bass foundation, with the middle voices often shrivelling up into chords without any line of their own. Since the topmost voice is acoustically bound to dominate, and the middle part is too hemmed in to play much of an individual rôle, the treble instruments in the various family groups acquired greater prominence than hitherto. Indeed, families of instruments were no longer built as a matter of course. In some cases the medium-range and lower-range instruments disappeared altogether. A good example of this is the POMMER group whose only survivor was the treble instrument, the *haut-bois* (its big cousin, the *gros-bois*, going out of use altogether). In other families only the bass instrument kept going. This happened, for instance, with the DULZIANS, whose lowest member served as prototype for the bassoon, while the medium-range and treble members, which are technically unsuitable for solo work, fell out of favour. There were still other families which died out altogether. Such was the case with the CRUMHORNS whose restricted compass and lack of expressiveness made them unsuitable for late Baroque music.

On the other hand keyboard instruments which encouraged the soloist clearly increased in popularity. With them one player, on his own, can provide all the main and subsidiary voices. He has complete control of the whole tonal complex and can vary it at will, extending it or shortening it, speeding it up or slowing it down, as the fancy takes him.

In Italy nothing changed in the way harpsichords were constructed. Even large instruments had only one manual with two eight-foot stops. Since the frame was not loaded with other courses of strings the harpsichord could thus develop its maximum tonal beauty. Here, as in so many other fields, the Italians instinctively knew it was best to stick to 'classical' specifications.

In the collection of the Paris Musée Instrumental du Conservatoire National Supérieur de Musique there is a fine Italian-

56   The *Nürmbergisch Geigenwerk* by Sebald Haiden of Nuremberg. The strings are 'bowed' by parchment-covered wheels turned by a pedal action. A *Geigenwerk* was preferable to the clavichord because of its greater volume of sound, to the harpsichord because of its sustained tone, and to the organ because of its better dynamic range. Woodcut in Michael Praetorius' *Syntagma Musicum*, 1618.

55   *(opposite)* Trumpet by M. Nagel, 1657. The mottos and emblems reflect several aspects of Baroque life, in particular the high standing of the guild trumpeters [see also figures 87, 88].

47

57 *(opposite)* Rubens, *The Education of Marie de Medici.* Apollo is playing a viol and a theorbo lies on the ground beside him.

58 Harpsichord by Faby, 1677.

type harpsichord built by Faby, an instrument-maker from Bologna who had settled in Paris. Its rich decorations can be accounted for by the fact that it was intended for Count Hercule Pepoli, godson of Louis XIV, *le roi soleil*. In the middle of the ebony frontal board, adorned with all sorts of masks, garlands of

59 An English virginal by Adam Leversidge, 1666. The painting on the lid shows courtiers and elegantly dressed ladies strolling down the Mall in St James's Park, London.

60 *(opposite)* In this allegory of the creation of the world Athanasius Kircher, a learned Jesuit, compared the Creation with divine organ playing. Many old myths refer to the creation of the world from the *logos* of sound. The events of the six days of Creation are here represented by six stops from whose appropriate organ pipes the divine breath of life emerges. Beneath the keyboard there are the words *Sic ludit in orbe terrarum aeterna Dei sapientia* (Thus the eternal wisdom of God plays in the universe). Note the unusual disposition of 'black' and 'white' notes on the divine keyboard.

fruit and flowers, and landscape impressions in ivory, there is – also in ivory – the coat of arms of the Pepolis: a chessboard. Romeo Pepoli, head of the Guelphs in Bologna, had used this symbol at the beginning of the fourteenth century for a party he founded under the name *Scacchesi,* and the symbol came to be accepted as the family's armorial device. The frontal board is bounded at both ends by a swan standing on a chessboard. The inside of the side walls and the jack-rail are all richly inlaid. The edges of the body are studded with ivory knobs – an Italian peculiarity. The ivory and ebony keys are also richly decorated. The whole body is loosely inserted in a casing painted white, blue and brown in imitation marble [figure 58].

England's continuing adherence to the VIRGINALS is proved by an attractive instrument, dated 1666, from the hand of Adam Leversidge, adorned with paintings of people walking [figure 59].

Attempts to mechanize as many sound-producing operations as possible led to the invention of the GEIGENWERK, a sort of bowed keyboard which is presumably what Samuel Pepys meant when he wrote about an 'arched viall' in his Diary for 5 October, 1664. Ever since the ninth century the mechanization

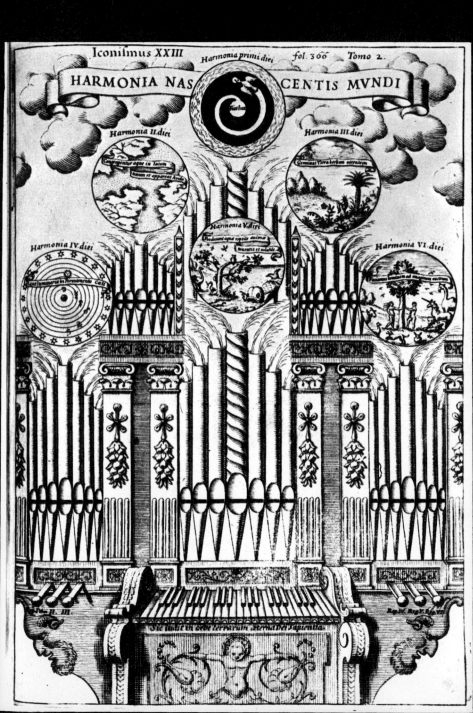

61 *Geigenwerk* by Raymundo Truchado, 1625, probably modelled on Haiden's instrument, though here the wheels are turned by a handle at the end of the instrument.

62 The musical contest between Apollo and Marsyas judged by King Midas, painted on the lid of a Venetian harpsichord of the late seventeenth century.

of string bowing had been practised with the hurdy-gurdy, an instrument that we shall examine more closely later in this book. However, the application of this principle to a keyboard instrument capable of playing chords did not take place until the early seventeenth century (although Leonardo da Vinci experimented with a *viola organista,* and Galilei reported something similar). In 1617 Praetorius gave an enthusiastic description of a *Geigenwerk* made by Sebald Haiden of Nuremberg [figure 56]. Five or six wheels covered with rosined parchment were turned by means of a pedal. The keys pressed the strings against the wheels. Bowed keyboards with similar mechanism were made by many instrument-makers in the seventeenth, eighteenth and nineteenth centuries. Even in our century experimental models are still being made. This makes it all the more strange that the device has never really made a name for itself, particularly since it has received the highest commendation from competent authorities. Carl Philipp Emanuel Bach, in the second part of his *Essay on the true art of playing keyboard instruments* (Berlin 1762), says 'it is a pity that Holfeld's invention of the ''bowed piano'' has not received general acceptance...One would certainly believe it to be highly valuable in accompanying'.

The *Geigenwerk* owned by the Brussels collection – made by Fra Raymundo Truchado, is more or less a copy of Haiden's instrument, although he describes himself as its *INVENTOR: 1625* [figure 61]. Victor-Charles Mahillon, founder of the Brussels collection, acquired the instrument in Madrid. The soundboard – painted in the Flemish manner – is unfortunately not original. Inside the lid there are two oil paintings which

63 Positive organ from Friesach in Carinthia, *c.* 1700. The cupboard-shaped
case is painted in red and green imitation marbling – Baroque *trompe l'oeil*.

64 Theorbo-player – from J.C. Weigel, *Musicalisches Theatrum, c.* 1700. In Baroque times the theorbo was one of the most important instruments for playing accompaniments.

65 Magnificent, almost living, layered rosette of a *chitarra battente* by Andreas Oth of Prague (1650–83).

are hardly likely to have been there originally either. One of them shows the rape of a nymph by two tritons; the other is a formal garden scene with a palace in the distance. The whole of the case is covered in purple velvet with the arms of the noble owner embroidered in gold and silk. An interesting feature is the position in which it was played – on the floor. We are told that 'the keyboard is only 34 centimetres [13½ inches] from the ground from which one can assume that the player would sit, oriental fashion, on a cushion to operate it. This is hardly surprising when one realizes that Spain retained some of the habits of its old Moorish conquerors until the beginning of the seventeenth century.'

The miniature organ also remained very popular. An Austrian positive from Friesach in Carinthia was originally built for playing in a domestic interior. Only later, during the eighteenth century, was it adapted by alterations to the pipes to playing in the open. Its new, more penetrating voice made it suitable for use in processional music. It is a four-foot instrument, i.e., like the octave spinet, it is pitched an octave higher than normal. In view of its small size this had distinct advantages, such as the fact that pipes did not have to be bent to fit them into the limited space available. The resulting tone is accordingly much more satisfactory. The bellows for providing the wind are on top of the instrument so that its 'breathing rhythm' can be seen as well as heard [figure 63].

The Týn church in Prague has a small Baroque processional organ with three stops. Until only a short while ago it was in use to accompany hymn singing in processions past the thirty statues of saints on the famous Charles Bridge.

Just as a king needs a court, and the sun its planets, so does a solo instrumental or vocal part need musical accompaniment. Ever since the sixteenth century instruments specially suitable for this purpose had been built. Among these was the bass-lute, usually referred to as the THEORBO. This had an extended neck with a second peg-box for the additional bass strings. In *Das neu eröffnete Orchester* (1713) Mattheson describes the theorbo as 'similar in many respects to the lute, especially as regards the body and, in part, the neck, only this is longer and has eight large bass strings which are twice as long and thick as the six of the lute. This renders the sound smooth and ringing so that many prefer the theorbo to a keyboard instrument because, they point out, it is easier to carry a theorbo to another place than a harpsichord', a purely practical consideration that certainly played a rôle.

This 'Paduan' theorbo differed from the 'Roman' theorbo – or CHITARRONE – in that the latter had a smaller body but a much longer neck, often more than twice as long as the actual body of the lute. These 'archlutes' were an essential component

in every court orchestra. In Vienna, for example, under Emperor Leopold I (who was himself a composer) the *Hofkapelle* employed two theorbo-players as well as a lutenist.

An exceptionally fine Venetian chitarrone of the late seventeenth century is owned by the Paris Conservatoire [figure 67]. The fingerboard and its extension above the first peg-box is adorned with intricate ebony and ivory inlaid work. We see the unfortunate huntsman Actaeon watching Diana and her companions bathing. Two of his hounds, who are shortly to devour him, bark at him while at his feet there lies a little monkey. The rest of the decoration is dominated by fantastic zoomorphic and anthropomorphic figures together with one curiously placid-looking *putto* playing a triangle.

It was also quite normal at the time for citterns to be 'theorbized', i.e., another neck and peg-box added so that additional bass strings could be incorporated. The results were often very strange, as can be seen from an instrument in the Vienna collection which was acquired in 1916 at an auction of the property of the painter Amerling. This highly ornamental cittern, curiously curved, has three star-decorated rosettes [figure 70].

The Musée du Conservatoire in Paris has a cittern, presumably of the early seventeenth century, which is distinguished by its elegantly carved head of a lady who seems to lean forward intent on hearing the instrument she graces [figure 71].

In the seventeenth century the GUITAR seems to have come into favour in Paris thanks to the Italian comedians, and as a fashionable instrument in aristocratic circles it was lavishly decorated. The Paris Conservatoire has a splendid instrument, also with ebony and ivory intarsio, which was made for Mademoiselle de Nantes in 1687 by the Parisian *luthier* Alexandre Voboam [figure 66]. (Mlle de Nantes was one of the eight children born to the vivacious Marquise de Montespan during her eight-year liaison with Louis XIV.)

As far as bowed instruments went the viol family still dominated the scene. The upstart VIOLIN somehow did not catch on in polite circles. 'The violin is too crude', said Mersenne in his theoretical treatise *Harmonie universelle* (1636); and the Hon. Roger North, a London lawyer under Charles II and James II, wrote disparagingly: 'the use of the violin had bin litle in

66 Guitar made by the Parisian *lithier* Voboam in 1687 for Mlle de Nantes, an illegitimate daughter of Louis XIV. It is still kept in its original case decorated with a coat of arms and fleurs-de-lis.

67 Late seventeenth-century chitarrone with intarsio work showing Diana bathing, surprised by Actaeon. The little monkey at his feet was a contemporary symbol for *imprudentia*, as well as for *astucia ingannevole*, deceptive cunning.

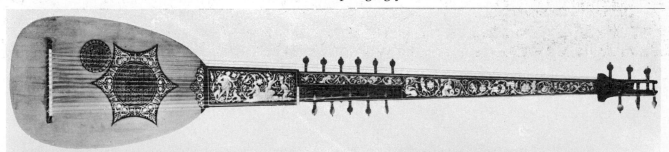

68 *Children Making Music*, 1629, by the Flemish painter Jan Miense Molenaer. In the seventeenth century the violin was looked on as a socially inferior instrument, and here it is ranged with the most vulgar sort of noise-producing objects. In the middle of the picture spoons are being drummed on a helmet, and on the right a *rommelpot* is being sounded. This is a friction-drum which is used in certain mystical African initiation rites and is still sometimes played in Holland as a joke instrument.

69 Page from a Baroque writing primer showing patterns for the letter N. Except in Italy, the violin was long considered an instrument fit only for professional musicians, not for polite society.

70 *(below left)* Theorbized cittern with body of extremely unusual shape. Possibly of early seventeenth-century Scandinavian origin.

71 *(below centre)* Cittern dating from the early seventeenth century. The crown-shaped pegs are extremely rare.

72 *(below right)* Guitar by Joachim Tielke, 1703, inlaid with tortoiseshell and ivory, made for a Danish princess.

England except by comon fidlers'. The result was that the viols (played *da gamba,* i.e., between the legs) were nearly always richly adorned, whereas the violins (played *da braccio,* on the arm) were generally very simple in outward appearance, without frets and having only four strings.

Joachim Tielke, probably the most famous *luthier* of the Late Baroque period, also made some very fine viols. His TENOR VIOL in the Claudius Collection in Copenhagen is exceptionally elegant. The ebony and ivory fingerboard includes, among its floral motifs, the figure of Hercules standing on the Lernaean Hydra just after he has been hit by a dart from the winged Cupid [figure 74].

Considerably more restrained in their execution than Tielke's viols were those made in London by Barak Norman. These were skilfully constructed instruments, mostly with discreet stylized ornamentation in inlaid wood [figure 73].

One country appears always to have held the violin in high esteem: Italy. This classical violin-building land early realized

73 *(opposite)* Bass viol by Barak Norman, London, 1723. Almost all his instruments have stylized ornaments in attractive wooden inlay.

74 The costly workmanship of this viol by Joachim Tielke indicates that it was made for an aristocratic amateur. The figures of Hercules and Cupid on the fingerboard are separated by the motto *VIRTVTIS RADIX AMOR* (The root of virtue is love). All Tielke's instruments are superb examples of craftsmanship and tonal quality.

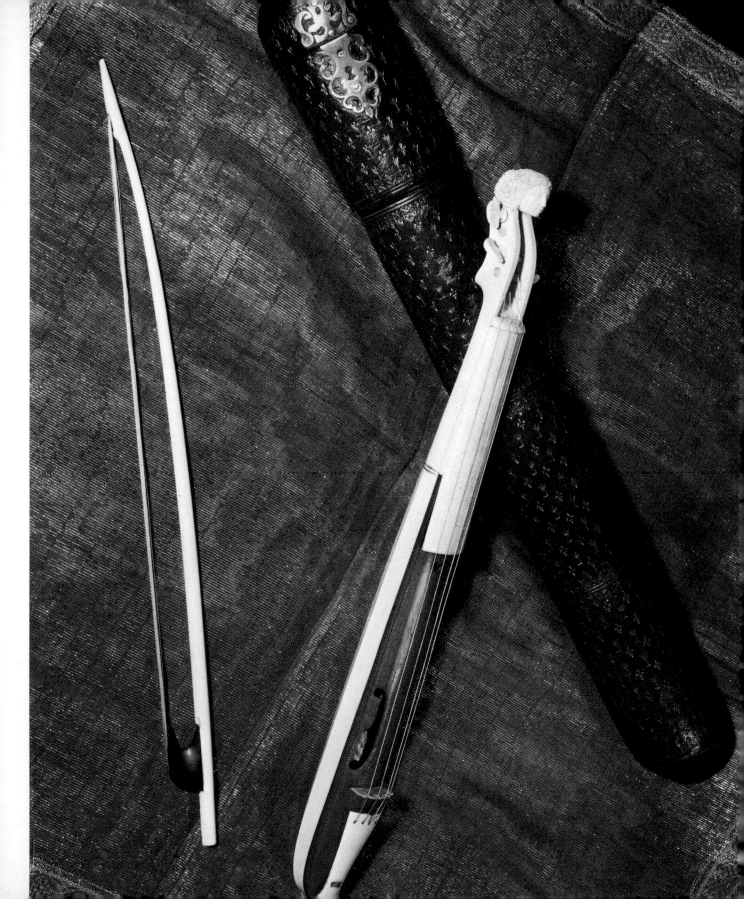

77 Kettle-drums as depicted by Caspar Majer in his *Museum Musicum*, 1732. Baroque kettle-drums were played with wooden sticks, and the tone was more penetrating than that produced with modern felt heads.

the expressiveness of the violin and gave it an important place in fashionable music-making. The outstanding Italian craftsman in this field was Antonio Stradivari who lived in Cremona, the world's most renowned centre for violin-making. Stradivari served his apprenticeship there under Nicolo Amati, perhaps the greatest member of a whole family of violin-makers. Strangely enough, although Stradivari's achievements were widely recognized during his lifetime – his customers included the Dukes of Savoy and Modena, Cardinal Orsini, the Elector of Saxony and other notables – preference was generally expressed for violins by Amati and by Jacob Stainer, an Austrian under strong Italian influence. Only after his death did Stradivari acquire real renown. Paganini and Viotti brought his violins international fame. Their material value then rose astonishingly. Whereas Stradivari had sold his instruments for about £4 or £5 ($10 to $15), their price had leapt by 1824 to £100, and in 1909 to between £500 and £1000. In 1953 a 'Strad' fetched £12,000 ($33,500) at W. E. Hill & Sons in London. About six hundred of the master's instruments are known to be still in existence. Those dating from the 'golden period' (approximately 1695–1725) are most highly prized. They are identifiable, among other features, by their specially fine dark red to amber varnish [figure 84].

The Rijksmuseum in Amsterdam has an amusing exhibit of curiosity value only. It is a violin in Delft faience whose scroll is

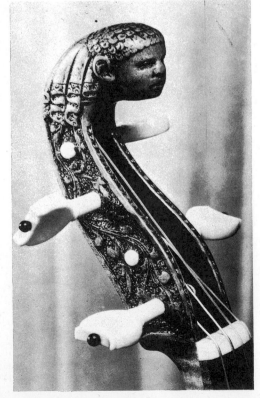

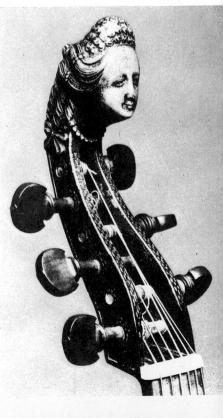

replaced by a striking bell-capped jester's head. He is an elderly man who eyes us roguishly. A *genre* picture (of a room where dancing is going on) covers the whole of the 'soundboard' [figure 75]. Experiments of this sort, inspired by the beauty of the instrument's shape, were not unusual and constituted a sort of musical *trompe l'oeil*.

Mattheson tells us about another rarity in this field, 'the hoarse and homely walking stick fiddle' which 'has been wholly appropriated by the dancing-master'. This was the POCHETTE, a tiny 'kit' violin, generally long, narrow and boat-shaped, which could, conceivably, have fitted into a rather large pocket. The pochette was a survival of the REBEC which had declined from being a medieval angelic attribute to a handy accompaniment for seventeenth-century dancing lessons. In 1628 and 1648 the Paris *lieutenant civil* ordained that the only bowed instrument permissible in the city's *cabarets* and *mauvais lieus* was the rebec. Today, too, there are instruments which it is taken for granted are reserved for specific surroundings and are practically barred from concert use, e.g., accordion, mouth organ, saxophone, Hammond organ, etc. The tone of the pochette was small but sufficiently penetrating for it to be used as a rhythmical basis in a dancing class. The one natural characteristic of the raucous rebec had found a worthy outlet.

Another curious instrument with strictly limited use was the TROMBA MARINA — otherwise known as the *Trumscheit* (drum-

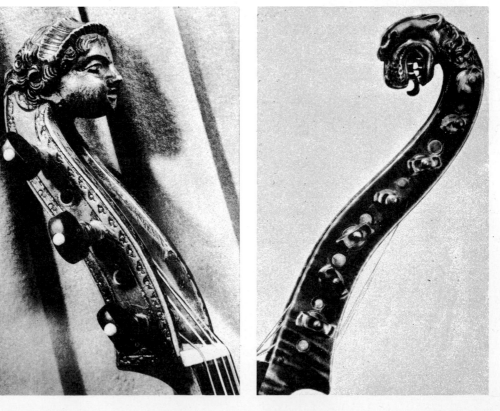

log) or *Nonnengeige* (nun's fiddle) – a single-string instrument which, as the name implies, could stand in for the trumpet. The tromba marina is usually of man's height. It has an extremely short neck and an asymmetrical shoe-shaped bridge with only one end fixed to the soundboard. The other vibrates with the string and drums on the belly, reinforcing the effect of the bowed sound [figure 86]. In Baroque times and later it was played only by making use of the string's natural harmonics, thus enhancing the trumpet effect. The earliest known pictorial representation of the tromba marina is in a French carving of the twelfth century. The last ones to be made date from the nineteenth century.

The whole history of the instrument, its music and its players, is rather obscure. When it stood in for the trumpet (as it often did in churches and nunneries where the guild-linked trumpeters were generally frowned upon) then its literature would have been identical with that of the trumpet. In spite of its long, active history, original works for tromba marina are few and far between. However, a certain Lorenzo de Castro did actually write a *Sonata per Tromba Marina* in the seventeenth century, and a contemporary of his, Johann Melchior Gletle, *Kapellmeister* of Augsburg Cathedral, published a series of 'trumpet pieces' (clearly meant for the tromba marina) in his *Musica genialis latino-germanica*, 1671. These were obviously occasional works since the collection is subtitled 'for table music during distinguished meals and other gay assemblies'. In keeping with the typical Baroque mood each of the short duets is given a motto derived from classical antiquity (with a suitable musical interpretation). Star-gazing *Hesperus* is represented by a gently swinging adagio; the restless, goat-footed *Fauns* have a hopping rhythm with dotted notes; *Heat or Ardour which inflames the Passions* is heralded by a stirring fanfare – and so on.

In France the tromba marina seems to have been highly appreciated alongside the crumhorn, which had been revived there after a long period of neglect. As from 1679 we find both the crumhorn and the tromba marina listed among the instruments played by the *Bande de la grande Ecurie du Roi de France* each of whose twenty-five members was expected to be proficient in two instruments. This court band was employed 'to play at hunts and processions and altogether on every occasion where music was needed in the open air'. Since the ensemble included musettes, flutes, oboes, side-drums and kettle-drums, as well as trumpets, the presence of a tromba marina player must presumably be accounted for by his curiosity value, and not because he had to substitute for a trumpeter. Tromba marina players were still listed in the royal band at the end of the eighteenth century. Lully, in his opera *Xerxes*, 1660, scored for two tromba marina players in the ballet music for a sailor's

83 *(opposite)* Baryton by Jacques Sainprae, Berlin, *c.* 1720. The baryton was a cross between a cello and a chitarone – bowed and without frets on the fingerboard, but with a number of sympathetic strings, which greatly increased its resonance. It was still used in the early nineteenth century, and Schubert composed music for baryton.

84 *Messie* violin, 1716, by Antonio Stradivari of Cremona, the most important centre in the world of classical violin-building. The violin has retained its classical, balanced shape practically unchanged since the sixteenth century. The scroll which still terminates the peg-box is a typical Baroque feature. The *Messie* is one of the most famous of all violins, the instrument and varnish being in mint condition.

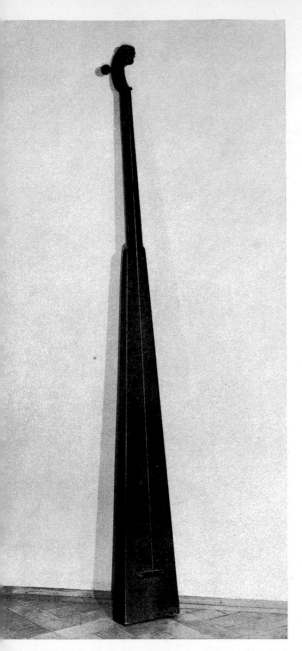

85 Tromba marina of the late seventeenth century. The sole decorative feature of its simple but distinguished design is the finely carved lion's head at the top.

87, 88 *(opposite)* Details of mottos and emblems of M. Nagel's trumpet [figure 55]: *(left)* 'Wax and grow in God' (Palm reaching up to heaven); *(right)* 'No storm wind can harm thee' (Tower being assailed by the four winds).

dance. We can assume that Molière wished his *Bourgeois Gentilhomme*, M. Jourdain, to demonstrate his lack of good taste when he proclaims: 'The tromba marina is an instrument that pleases me and is harmonious.' On the other hand the *London Gazette* of 4 February, 1674 announces 'a rare concert of four trumpets marine, never heard of before in England', and adds: 'If any persons desire to come and hear it, they may repair to the Fleece Tavern, near St James's about two of the clock in the afternoon, every day in the week except Sundays. Every concert shall continue one hour, and so begin again. The best places are one shilling, and the others sixpence.'

Of course, the genuine flourish of a TRUMPET can never be replaced by another instrument, whether cornett, tromba marina or anything else. The Baroque period was one long display of pomp and circumstance and on no important occasion could the trumpet be missing. The shimmer of its silvery sound was an essential part of marriages and memorials, receptions, processions and festivities of every kind. All the world really was a stage, and its players were musicians. The trumpeter had many other vital functions to fulfil too. In the field of battle the trumpet was the best means of signalling; and nothing could conceivably be more fitting to proclaim the arrival of an ambassador. In the Holy Roman Empire and in Germany trumpeters regarded themselves as a cut above all the other musicians. In 1623 they obtained special privileges in a decree issued by Emperor Ferdinand II. The guild system was so strongly enforced that aspirants had to learn the art of playing from members. These saw to it that the trumpet was not performed on any 'unworthy occasion', and that it was not used by any 'town-pipers, minstrels or comedians' who were not initiated into the 'noble art of trumpeting'. There was only one instrument with which the trumpet deigned to ally itself and that was the KETTLE-DRUM. The kettle-drummers too had been granted an Imperial Privilege and so held the same status as trumpeters in the 'heroic' Guild of Court and Field Trumpeters and Court and Army Kettle-Drummers. Their glorious music was never missing on important occasions in any princely household. The bands of today's cavalry regiments reflect this pageantry to some extent.

Although the trumpets normally played in six parts the fact that only one of them was usually written out (and thus preserved) can be accounted for by the guild system since the other players automatically knew how they were supposed to improvise. Only on rare occasions were all six voices put down *in extenso*, one example being Schmelzer's music for the Horse Ballet given at the court of Vienna in 1667 on the occasion of Leopold I's marriage to the Infanta Margareta. The spectacle was watched by the Emperor himself on horseback attended by all his cavaliers.

Tromba Marina

86 Tromba marina player. The strings are stopped very lightly with the fingers because only the natural harmonics are played. Engraving in Filippo Bonanni's *Gabinetto Armonico*, Rome, 1722.

The Vienna collection houses a particularly fine instrument by Michael Nagel which displays the proud circumstances of its original purpose. It is made of silver with engraved ornamentation and gilt trimmings. The bell is decorated with the carved heads of cherubs, and the knob on the shaft is in the shape of a lion's head. The trumpet is marked *MICHAEL NAGEL/ NVERNBERG 1657* together with a monogram 'MN' and a bird. It was obviously not an instrument for everyday use; these were made of brass. The use of silver had special significance. Hanns Neuschel, for instance, went to Rome himself to deliver (and play) the silver trombones he had made for Pope Leo x. The alchemist's lore recognized silver as *albicans et sonorum* (shimmering and sonorous) and attributed to it a quality of 'bright gaiety' [figures 55, 87, 88]. Another trumpet from Nagel's workshop (dated 1654) is in Lübeck, and the Bayerisches Nationalmuseum in Munich has a tenor trombone of 1656.

One of the most widely used melody instruments of Baroque times was certainly the RECORDER, otherwise known as the *flûte à bec* or the *flûte douce* – attributes which Johann Friedrich Bernhard Caspar Majer tells us, in *Museum Musicum*, come 'firstly from its mouthpiece which looks like a bird's beak and secondly from its subdued charm'. Towards the end of the seventeenth century the recorder underwent several internal changes to fit it better for playing solos, and the body acquired ornate swellings which upset the stern simplicity of the original tubular shape. The mouthpiece and the flange at the bottom were also given a more pronounced shape. Whereas the earlier recorder had rather thick walls with a wide, almost cylindrical, bore, it now adopted thin walls and a narrow, conical bore. These alterations, together with modifications to the fipple and the 'lip', increased the instrument's range in the overblown

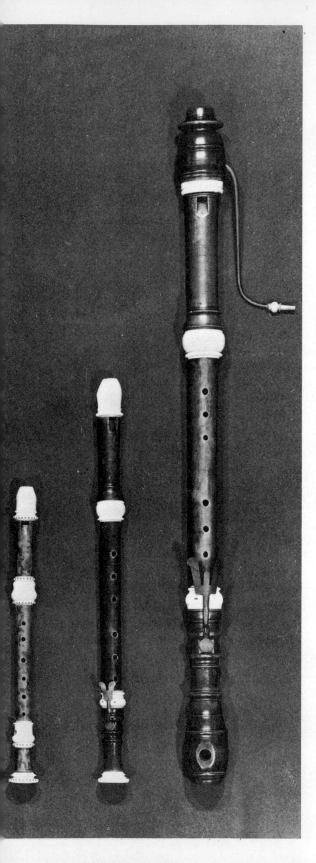

FLÛTE DOUSE.

Des Klanges süßigkeit zeigt schon der Flöten-nahme.
die dient zur Courtoisie bey Sternen voller Nacht.
Sie ists die offt bewegt, manch angenehme Dame
wann ihr ein Ständgen wird bey stiller ruh gebracht
das Sie des Sanfften Betts, Sich offt wohl gar entziehet
und zu dem Süßen thon, hin an das Fenster fliehet.

89 (opposite left) Baroque recorders (treble, tenor and bass). The quiet simplicity of the older sort of one-piece recorders disappeared in the seventeenth century. In its place the Baroque recorder appeared in a three-part construction with bulbous joints. Although not made entirely of ivory they were generally decorated with ivory collars or spats.

90 (opposite right) Treble recorder player. During the High Baroque the treble recorder acquired a dominant position as the solo instrument of the recorder family. Its characteristic sweetness of tone was reflected in names such as *flauto dolce, flûte douce,* etc. The verse beneath the player extols the efficacy of the recorder as a serenading instrument.

91 Fish-faced treble recorders made of wood and ivory.

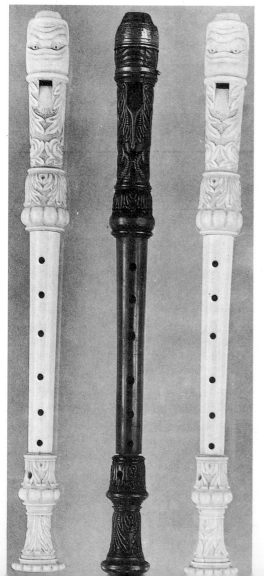

octave as well as making this part of the compass easier to obtain with correct intonation. This advantage was obtained at the expense of the lower notes, however, which lost some of their fullness and roundness – an example of the law of compensation which Goethe expressed so succinctly in his *Metamorphosis of the Animals*:

'These frontiers are stretched by no god; Nature honours them:
For only within limits is perfection possible ...
And should you see one creature to whom particular advantage
Has been granted then ask at once: Where does it suffer
Other shortcomings? ...'

The Baroque recorder only develops its real charm in its upper, 'falsetto' octave, where the sound is brighter and more rich in overtones. These characteristics conformed with the new approach to music with its emphasis on virtuoso brilliance. In every respect the Baroque ideal – whether in architecture, painting or music – seemed to be sparkle and luminosity. The trend was towards the white, gold and delicate pastel shades of the Rococo around the corner.

Just as in the other families of instruments so, too, in the recorder group one member – the treble recorder – emerged as the solo instrument *par excellence* [figure 90]. As from the end of the seventeenth century the recorder became increasingly fashionable among amateurs. To satisfy their eyes as well as their ears the finest possible wood was used for the recorder as well as 'clear ivory' (which was regarded as being on a plane with gold, silver and precious stones when it came to producing costly works of applied art). A comparatively large number of ivory recorders have been preserved, perhaps because their inherent value saved them from the fate of their lesser, wooden, brothers and sisters. Top and bottom joints of the recorder were often adorned with carving. One ivory flute belonging to the Musée Instrumental du Conservatoire National Supérieur de Musique in Paris has a mouthpiece resembling the head of a fish whose eyes stare at the player. The rest of the decoration is in the form of beautiful acanthus leaves. Other 'fish-face' flutes are generally made of wood. They correspond to a Baroque leaning towards the grotesque which, in its turn, has overtones of the playful magic which can breathe life into inanimate objects [figure 91].

Rococo

92 Clavicytherium by Albert Delin, second half of the eighteenth century, with characteristic *rocaille* ornaments.

THE TREND TOWARDS MONODY CONTINUED during the periods of Rococo and Classicism – inasmuch as those had a distinctive musical identity. In certain essential respects the approach naturally differed. The sometimes massive pomposity of the Baroque age – which, in fact, behind its ecstasy and all its lush verdure was only the outer trappings of a clear, symmetrical structure – gradually assumed a gracious weightlessness, waiting to take off, as it were, on a cloud of *petits riens*. This transformation was reflected by the outward appearance of the musical instruments of the time.

Perhaps one of the most characteristic examples is the CLAVICYTHERIUM made by Albert Delin of Tournai which is now in the collection of the Gemeentemuseum in The Hague [figure 92]. Basically this is a harpsichord whose strings are disposed vertically instead of horizontally. The mechanism is, of course, more complicated because the jacks cannot fall back of their own weight but have to be pushed back into place by metal springs. Its main advantage was its size. Athanasius Kircher tells us in his well-known *Musurgia*: 'Instruments of this sort are in great demand in Germany; they are convenient because they take up little space, and are also decorative in the rooms.' It is difficult to decide just when the clavicytherium first came into being. The usual examples quoted are the illustration of such an instrument in Sebastian Virdung's *Musica getutscht und aussgezogen* (1511), and the instrument in London's Royal College of Music which can hardly be later than the first years of the sixteenth century [figure 94]. However, before the end of the fifteenth century a small portable clavicytherium was depicted in the hands of an angel on the magnificent carved altarpiece at Kefermarkt in Upper Austria.

The clavicytherium in The Hague – just like the two other known instruments by Albert Delin (in Berlin and Brussels) – has its soundboard covered with floral motifs. Its attractive rosette shows a harp-playing angel between the initials *AD*. The case of the clavicytherium is white offset with gold, a combination that is very typical of the Rococo period. All thought of symmetry is dispersed by the exuberant ornamentation whose intertwining strands of rank vegetation threaten to engulf the instrument. The soundboard itself disappears entirely beneath a mass of intricate carving amidst which we can discern patches of blossoming flowers and groups of miniature instruments. The principle of the clavicytherium lived on in such instruments as the 'giraffe piano' and the 'pyramid piano' and is still employed today in the pianino.

Among the other keyboard instruments the greatest favourite during the eighteenth century was the CLAVICHORD. With its delicate, intimate tone, capable of the most subtle expression, it answered perfectly another musical need of the period: sensibility. Weary of the Cartesian *clara et distincta perceptio*, where reason reigned supreme, sentiment was allowed, encouraged, to come to the fore. An escape was sought in the beautiful clarity of melting feelings, quitting the bright geometry of the intellect for the protective twilight of the heart. It was the first hint of the Romantic Age that was to come. As a counterpart to the playful frivolity of the Rococo this was its genuinely heartfelt aspect.

93 Violin and cello players in a Rococo landscape. As can be seen, ornamentation had penetrated into every sphere of life. Engraving by J. R. Holzhalb, *Musikalische Neujahrsgeschenke,* Zurich, 1761.

94 The earliest known clavicytherium that has been preserved, early sixteenth century. One of the sound-holes is decorated with a Gothic tracery window-frame.

The inherent delicacy of the sound produced by the clavichord was exploited during the Rococo period as a positive characteristic. An attempt was even made to find an unusual explanation for the name. The German scholar Jakob Adlung saw this possibility: 'The clavichord gets its name from *chorda*, a string, and *clavis*, a key, or from *cor*, the heart, a derivation which can be supported by the fact that the proper clavicord [sic], when properly played, stirs the heart more deeply than almost any other instrument.' The clavichord was indeed highly esteemed in eighteenth-century Germany, which was sometimes claimed as the 'true home' of what the poet Schubart called 'this lonely, melancholy, indescribably sweet instrument' [figure 95].

The clavichord was still the only keyboard instrument on which a performer could execute delicate dynamic changes. The pianoforte was only just beginning to put in an appearance and took a long time to catch on. And even on the pianoforte (or *Hammerklavier* as it was at first called in German-speaking countries) it was not possible to influence a note once it had been struck. On the clavichord a sort of controlled vibrato could be produced. In his *Essay* Carl Philipp Emanuel Bach recommends the use of *Bebung* on 'long and emotional notes' through 'rocking the finger evenly on the key'. Schubart considered that on the clavichord

it is possible to determine not only the predominant musical colour but also the shading, the swelling and the intention of the notes, the trill that melts under the fingers, the *portamento* or carrying power – indeed every feature that creates the emotional effect. Anyone who is not fond of bluster, haste and storm, whose heart is full of sweet sentiment, should avoid the harpsichord and the pianoforte and choose a clavichord.

C. P. E. Bach was himself a highly gifted performer on the clavichord. A contemporary reported that he was not only capable of playing 'quite a slow, singing adagio with the most

touching expression to the disgrace of many [professional] instrumentalists who should be able to imitate the voice with much greater ease', but he could also hold long notes 'with all different degrees of strength and weakness'. For the connoisseurs of his day he wrote his spirited sonatas, fantasias and rondos for clavichord, thus ensuring himself a place among the great lyricists of the keyboard.

Particularly fine clavichords were made in Hamburg. 'Here', wrote Mattheson, 'there are people who send clavichords every year, as many as they can make, to England, to Spain, to Holland etcetera.' Among the best builders was Johann Adolph Hass. The Musikhistorisk Museum in Copenhagen has a clavichord signed *J. A. HASS, HAMB ANNO 1755*. This is an unfretted instrument (i.e., there is a separate pair of strings – triple in the bass – for every note on the keyboard) of costly finish. The lower keys are covered with ivory, the upper ones with tortoiseshell

95 German fretted clavichords, eighteenth century; *(left)* instrument by Johann Weiss, 1702, *(below)* instrument with lid removed. In fretted instruments each string, by serving more than one tangent, is used for two or three notes.

97 Hallelujah allegory. An almost explosive bunch of instruments – viol, violin, harp, lute, recorder, flute, oboe, bassoon, horns, trumpets and kettle-drums. On the left a large, but simply-shaped harpsichord, and an organ with painted wings, showing King David playing the harp. Engraving made by J. R. Holzhalb, Zurich, 1759.

(and ivory ornaments). The case is painted bright red and inside the cover there is a fashionable *chinoiserie* landscape. (This pseudo-Romantic attraction for distant exotic *maraviglia* set in before the Rococo period, but it was only during the latter that it really came into its own. The acknowledged starting signal was the ball given by Louis XIV at Marly which opened with a *divertissement* entitled *Le Roy de la Chine*. Louis XV's favourite Château de la Muette was furnished from top to bottom in Chinese style. That the taste has never died out entirely is proved by stage works of Gilbert and Sullivan, Puccini, Lehár, and Britten.) The gentle yellow and green shades of the painting beneath the lid form a welcome contrast to the brilliant red of the case. The soundboard is strewn with painted flowers [figure 96].

Also in Copenhagen, in the Collection of Carl Claudius, there is a positive organ, of south German origin, with attractive carving [figure 98]. The instrument proper, with its ranks of pipes and their mechanism, is separate from the bellows box on which it stands. The *rocaille* 'curtain' permits a glimpse of the wooden pipes in their diminishing order of size. 'An eight-foot *Gedackt* (stopped rank) is certainly desirable for music, and anyway I regard it as essential for all positives', said Adlung in *Musica Mechanica Organoedi* (1768). On the inside of the doors there is the usual painted collection of instruments, including recorders, cornetts, oboes, viols, a tromba marina, bassoons, a serpent (the lowest member of the cornett family) and lutes. The pediment is topped with a delightful carved ornament in the centre of which there is a painted medallion showing St Cecilia, the patroness of music, playing a positive. The bellows chest is also richly ornamented, and has a pedal which can be operated by the player himself, thus obviating the need to engage an extra blower. Treading these bellows with the feet, however, necessitates a good deal of practice if the movement is to remain independent of the hands that are playing. Once this procedure has been mastered a much more organic effect can be achieved than with a mechanical blower.

In the latter part of the century England came to the fore in the final phase of harpsichord-building. It is almost possible to sense the struggle that was in progress to justify the instrument's existence. The compass was extended beyond five octaves. All sorts of stops were incorporated (Lute, Nasal, Harp and Buff – using leather 'quills'). Sometimes these registers were operated by 'machine stops' through pedals, instead of the hand action that had previously been standard. An attempt was also made to conquer the harpsichord's lack of dynamic adjustability by adding a 'Venetian swell' and other shutter devices.

The Swiss-born Burkat Shudi and his son-in-law John Broadwood, as well as Jacob Kirckman (from Alsace), were the principal English harpsichord-makers up till 1800. The Benton

98 South German
positive organ,
mid-eighteenth
century.

99 Harpsichord by Jacob and Abraham Kirckman, London, 1777, made of cross-banded mahogany, inlaid with strips of boxwood and ebony. The two manuals have 'white' keys of ivory, and 'black' keys of ebony. It is a typical instrument as made during the last age of harpsichord-building: the exterior already displays Classicist sobriety but there is no hint yet of the stiff elegance of early Classicism. Rococo as such never got a real foothold in Britain.

101 Ruckers harpsichord (1573) in an ornate Rococo case.

100 Rococo procelain group. The nobleman plays to his attentive lady on a *chitarra battente,* an Italian variant of the guitar with a curved back.

Fletcher Collection of Early Keyboard Instruments in Fenton House, Hampstead, London, has a number of fine harpsichords by Shudi and Kirckman which are outwardly very similar. They are all instruments of considerable size, their bodies generally veneered in mahogany or walnut, sometimes incorporating strips of boxwood and ebony. The whole appearance is strictly rectilinear – heavy, straight and sober – with all roundness avoided. As from 1772 Jacob Kirckman's instruments are jointly signed by his nephew Abraham. One of their joint productions (inscribed *JACOBVS ET ABRAHAM KIRCKMAN LONDINI FECERUNT 1777*) has a pedal on the right that engages the Nag's Head Swell, which, we are told, is 'a flap in the lid that produces a gradual crescendo effect' [figure 99].

Notwithstanding these efforts to give it artificially a range of expressiveness and dynamics comparable with that of the clavichord or the ascendant pianoforte, the harpsichord was fated to be eclipsed.

Classicism

103 Allegories of music and geometry, from an early nineteenth-century engraving. The figure of Music holds a lyre, a motif constantly found in the decoration of instruments of the Classicist period.

102 *(opposite)* Harp-lyre by Carlo Scalfi, early nineteenth century, one of the most attractive Classicist instruments. The arms of the yoke support round discs depicting the moon in a blue, starlit sky, and the sun in female personification. The sides of this glorious instrument are covered with stylized gilt foliage.

THE FLORID MISCHIEVOUSNESS OF THE ROCOCO was gradually restrained by a revival of interest in the tenets of classical antiquity. Lavish embellishment gave way to a stern insistence on structural purity. Clarity of outline was given preference over decoration. This applied just as much to music as to all the other arts. The ornamentation that had at times almost completely obscured the melodic line was progressively discarded. The underlying desire for natural simplicity meant a return to tunes with four-square folksong-like structure.

Old instruments were altered – inside and out – so as to comply with the new conception. A good example is the harpsichord by Andreas Ruckers (1640) in the Paris Conservatoire Collection which was rebuilt by Pascal Taskin in 1780. Taskin (who held the post of *garde des instruments du roi* from 1781–90) was one of France's leading harpsichord-makers. He increased the compass of Ruckers' original two-manual instrument by several notes at both ends of the keyboard, a process called *ravalement* which became accepted practice. Rousseau describes the *ravalement* system as 'one which, instead of limiting the keyboard to four octaves, extends it to five'. This extension of the range of keyboard instruments had, in fact, started during the Middle Ages and is still in progress. Whereas the inside of the lid of the harpsichord by Ruckers and Taskin retained its seventeenth-century painting, the colouring of the case and the stand on which it rests is strictly late eighteenth-century [figure 104].

However (until its revival in our own time) the harpsichord's days were numbered. Its earnest, even stately, tone was too lavish; its dynamic range was too restricted for pre-Romantic taste. Great masters of music, such as Haydn and Mozart – who started by using the harpsichord, turned increasingly to the PIANOFORTE which was to replace it entirely. The rise of the pianoforte provides a good example of the principle that an instrument generally only comes to the fore when it answers the acoustic needs of a particular age. Mechanization by keys of the dulcimer – which is what the pianoforte represents in all essentials – had long been in the air but was not developed. In other spheres the process had been started, or completed, much earlier.

Hydraulos, the water-organ of the ancients, was available

104 Harpsichord by
Andreas Ruckers, 1640,
rebuilt by Pascal Taskin. The
decoration on the case was
completely altered to suit
Classicist taste. The pseudo-
antique ornamentation is
based on Pompeian
grotesque figures and
wall-mouldings.

105 *(opposite)* Mechanical
trumpeter by Friedrich
Kaufmann, Dresden, 1810;
an automatic instrument
with tongues that are
activated by the usual pins
on a roller. Ever since
Renaissance times automatic
instruments have exercised a
mysterious fascination, and
have survived in Swiss
musical boxes and cuckoo
clocks.

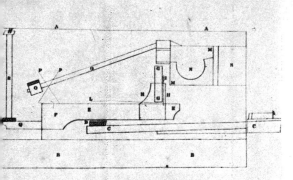

106 The first known illustration of a *Hammerklavier* mechanism by the Marchese Maffei, 1711. The possibility this provided of making dynamic gradations – coupled with a sheer volume of sound that the clavichord could never approach – soon brought the instrument the characteristic name of 'pianoforte'.

107 Square piano by Benjamin Crehore of Milton. In America the square piano achieved widespread popularity.

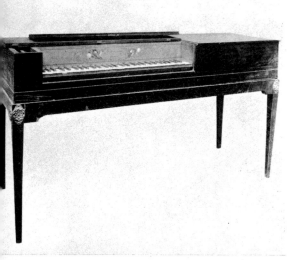

for wind music. Strings were being mechanically bowed (in hurdy-gurdies) by the tenth century at the latest. Key-operated plectrums plucked strings from at least the fifteenth century onwards. The clavichord, which had presumably been in existence since the twelfth century, combined the string-division system of the monochord with the striking principle of the dulcimer, although the tangent *remained in contact* with the string until the key was released. From here it would seem to have been only a short step to mechanizing the normal beater-action of the dulcimer player. A move in this direction was clearly taken by the *dulce melos.* This was a stringed keyboard instrument (described in a fifteenth-century Latin manuscript now in the Paris Bibliothèque Nationale) where the strings were struck vertically from below. The 'swinging' action of the pianoforte hammer had yet to be invented.

Not until about 1698, at the Medici court in Florence, was the pianoforte in its modern form 'invented' by Bartolomeo Cristofori. According to the latest research done by Mario Fabbri it was in that year that the harpsichord-maker Cristofori began, at the behest of Ferdinando dei Medici, to build keyboard instruments which were capable of 'speaking like the heart – sometimes with the delicate touch of an angel, at others with a violent burst of passion', as Giovanni M. Casini put it. By 1700 Ferdinando dei Medici's inventory of musical instruments describes 'an *arpicembalo* of Bartolomeo Cristofori, a new invention, which plays piano and forte . . . with some dampers of red cloth touching the strings and some hammers which make the piano and forte'. That these first instruments were, technically speaking, tremendously advanced can be judged from the illustrated description given by the Marchese Maffei in 1711 [figure 106]. All the same, composers for a long time took no notice of this advance. In addition to his instrument *col piano e forte* (thus stressing its dynamic possibilities) Cristofori went on building the usual sort of harpsichord with plucking action. No more success, either, was accorded the *clavecins à maillets* submitted by the Frenchman Marius to the Académie Royale in 1716.

The Italian invention was adopted in Germany by Gottfried Silbermann, and it was he who made the first German pianofortes. Frederick the Great, himself a composer and flute-player of no mean achievements, seems to have been a great admirer of this novelty, and acquired several splendid Silbermann pianofortes. Johann Sebastian Bach, when he visited the monarch at Potsdam, played the instruments and pronounced favourably on them. However, Bach could not have been very interested because, although he was friendly with Silbermann, he never himself ordered one of his pianofortes. Frederick the Great later became more attached to the harpsichord and never again bought a pianoforte. For a long time the pianoforte met bitter resistance. It was 'a noise-box where one note drums, another rattles, another buzzes, killing every feeling with hammers', as one, otherwise unknown, Silesian writer calling himself *Hermes junior* put it. In fact the pianofortes of Classicist times were unbelievably delicate and quiet compared with the pianos of our day. The construction was as light and elegant as that of the contemporary harpsichord.

It was not until the end of the century that the real breakthrough came with composers demanding an instrument that could not only convey delicate shades of dynamics but also produce enough volume for concertos. 'The pianoforte has in our days been refined and improved to such an extent that it is capable of expressing both what the harpsichord and the clavichord could do separately', wrote Bossler in *Musikalische Correspondenz* (1791). Before long the typical rectangular shape of the clavichord was also being employed for the pianoforte. German pianoforte-makers who had lost business because of the Seven Years' War turned to England for custom – and were

108 In the latter half of the eighteenth century the square piano was created by applying the rectangular shape of the clavichord to the pianoforte. This square piano by Buntebart & Sievers, London, 1786, already has a pedal to lift the dampers, an attachment that has been retained by the piano to the present day and is in fact of real service only in later non-polyphonic music. A harpsichord feature that has been incorporated is the lute-stop, a special type of string-damping that produces a tone similar to that of a plucked lute.

109 The extraordinary, celestial sound, *acutissimus sonus*, which can be produced by rubbing a fingertip around the rim of a glass had attracted the attention of the Jesuit priest Athanasius Kircher as early as the seventeenth century. In his *Phonurgia*, 1673, he examined the phenomenon in some detail in a chapter entitled '*De prodigiosa sonorum vi et efficacia*' (The wondrous power and effect of sounds).

110 *(opposite)* Double-pedal harp with 43 strings by Sebastian Erard, London, early nineteenth century, with fine Classicist 'Antique' decoration. In the course of the eighteenth century the harp grew to favour as a 'polite' instrument for ladies, partly, no doubt, because of its decorative effect. It is still predominantly played by women, so that normally all-made orchestras are frequently forced to engage a female harp-player.

successful. A SQUARE PIANO, dated 'London 1786' by Buntebart & Sievers – now in the collection at The Hague – is of typical Classicist exterior. The painting on the lid shows an open-air gathering with loving couples elegantly disporting themselves on a lawn around an antique garden-vase. The party is being entertained by a gesticulating singer who is accompanied by a lutenist and a violin-player. It is Rococo in retreat. The instrument's case is of fine veneer, discreetly embellished with cordons. The base and the tapering legs have only a minimum of ornamental relief [figure 108].

It was in America, though, that the square piano made its greatest mark. It held its own for one hundred years – from the end of the eighteenth until the end of the nineteenth century, when it was supplanted by the pianino. Benjamin Crehore of Milton started by building harpsichords but turned afterwards to pianofortes in which field he became one of the leading American names. It is said that he produced some of the first copies of English square pianos. In 1819 he died in poverty in Milton. One of his many square pianos can now be seen in Pingree House in Salem, Massachusetts. Apart from a flower-ringed maker's sign and some discreet leafy medallions at the point where the tapering legs meet the body, all decoration is avoided. The whole effect is one of puritanical severity and functionalism [figure 107].

One of the strangest instruments to answer the then current fad for somnambulism, mesmerism, magnetism and the like was the GLASS HARMONICA. This was a musical adaptation of the party game whereby wine-glasses can be made to 'sing' by stroking their rims with a wet finger. Various names were given to this device in its earliest, simplest form – *verillon, Glasspiel,* musical glass – but it was not until the end of the eighteenth century that the principle was fully exploited. The 'tuning' of the glasses was effected by adding or removing water, although Kircher (in both *Musurgia* and *Phonurgia*) developed an interesting theory that the listener's temperament could be variously influenced by filling them with different liquids such as brandy, wine, distilled water, sea water or pump water. He maintained that by experimenting in this way the same sound might be made to induce a different humour: choler, sanguinity or phlegm! However, the first known virtuoso player on the instrument, an Irishman by the name of Richard Pockrich, stuck for his performance to 'twenty-six drinking-glasses tuned with spring water'.

In 1763 the statesman and physicist Benjamin Franklin mechanized the action of the instrument. A series of glass bowls of decreasing size were mounted on a horizontal spindle which could be rotated with the help of a pedal. Musical vibrations could then be produced by applying the finger to the edges of the

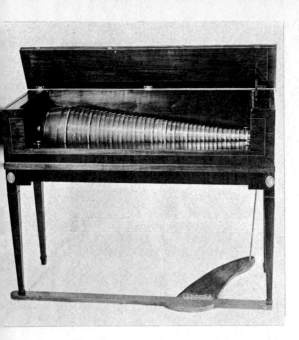

111 Glass harmonica of unknown origin, c. 1800. The glass bowls corresponding to the black keys on a piano are identified by their gold rims.

112 *(opposite)* The high status of the hurdy-gurdy in eighteenth-century France is demonstrated by the costly finish of this instrument, which belonged to Adélaïde, Madame de France, Louis xv's third daughter, and which is a mass of Classicist decoration. It is made of lemon-tree and box-wood and its colourful impression is enhanced still further by a fringe of mother-of-pearl medallions and inlaid turquoises. In spite of this lavish ornamentation Classicist symmetry and balance is fully retained.

bowls, if necessary to more than one at a time. Franklin's 'Armonica', as he himself called it, acquired several celebrated players, among them: Miss Marianne Davies, Messrs O. J. Frick, Naumann and C. F. Pohl senior; and, above all, the blind Marianna Kirchgessner (1770–1808) for whom Mozart in the last year of his life wrote an Adagio, K. 616a, and an Adagio and Rondo, K. 617 (with flute, oboe, viola and cello). Kirchgessner's playing was described enthusiastically by the *Hamburgischer Correspondent* (1792): 'Her adagio is ravishing and her allegro is admirable. She plays the instrument with such lightness that it is as if she had a keyboard beneath her fingers, performing grace-notes and trills which have hitherto been considered impossible.' It is interesting to note that Beethoven too once wrote for the instrument.

The delicate, yet penetrating, celestial sound is of uniquely mystifying magic. Just as in prehistoric times, sound *per se* is still able to enchant mankind. The didactic novel *Titan* (1800–03) by the German writer Jean Paul contains the following unforgettable analogy of the emotions aroused by what he calls this 'glassy sanctuary of the tonal muse':

The zephyr of sound, the harmonica, drifted sighingly over the garden blossom – and the notes cradled themselves in the thin lilies of the waking water so that the silver lilies burst for joy and sun into flame-like blossom.... Could you, Albano, keep happiness and sorrow hidden in your heart if you heard such a gentle virgin passing in the musical moonlight?

In the course of the nineteenth century the instrument slowly died out. Today we have another virtuoso of the glass harmonica, Bruno Hoffmann of Germany, whose performances have, fortunately, been recorded. He actually employs the old, pre-Franklin principle – with the hands rotating – since he considers this adds subtlety to the playing.

The glass harmonica in the Berlin collection dates from about 1800 but its maker is not known. The closely mounted pyramid of glass bowls is housed in a simple, rectangular mahogany case. The pedal, which drives the invisible flywheel inside through a belt, is mounted on a cross-bar fixed to the two front feet. The instrument has a compass of $3\frac{1}{2}$ octaves, corresponding to 44 glass bowls [figure 111].

Another fashionable eighteenth-century instrument, the HURDY-GURDY, is right at the other end of the aesthetic scale. Fondness for the sound of the hurdy-gurdy can be accounted for by another feature of the age: as yearning for the 'simple' life, for mock rusticality, with shepherds and shepherdesses in a pastoral idyll. Another instrument that came into this category was, of course, the bagpipes. The hurdy-gurdy, though, is a mechanized bowed instrument. The 'bow' is a resined wooden wheel which scrapes over the melody strings. These are stopped by keys with tangents. In addition to the usual pair of melody

strings (tuned in unison) the instrument has additional bourdons that provide a drone effect in the bass. Together this gives rise to one of the simplest and oldest forms of polyphony, a method still used in non-European music. (This stark contrast between a constant background noise and an irregular jumping movement always has an extraordinary effect on man. In the magical world of music as practised on some other continents it represents the struggle of good and evil, of life with death, as in the rites of the Bora Indians on the Amazon.)

At the same time the hurdy-gurdy is a noteworthy example of the manner in which an instrument's significance can change. In the Middle Ages one expected to see it gracing illustrations of angels and saints, but by the sixteenth century it was hardly being mentioned any more by the theorists, and in 1618 it had sunk in the eyes of Michael Praetorius to a 'revolving lyre for peasants and women'. In the eighteenth century it then came back for a sudden period of popularity in the highest social circles, only to sink again in the nineteenth to the level of a beggar's instrument and one for use in country bands. It is worth pointing out that the *Leiermann* in Schubert's sad song of the same name is a hurdy-gurdy player, as can be gathered from the character of the piano accompaniment. In the Paris *métro* one still occasionally encounters the hurdy-gurdy being played by an itinerant musician.

Like the medieval wheel of fortune – *Regno, sum sine regno* – what is treasured in one age is despised in another. What a curious stroke of fate that when the hurdy-gurdy was at the height of favour in the French upper classes (along with the *musette* or bagpipes) the violin was still considered beneath a gentleman's dignity! Even Voltaire was moved to write:

> O Chapelain! toi, dont le violon
> De discordante et gothique mémoire
> Sous un archet maudit par Apollon
> D'un ton si dur a raclé son histoire.

(Oh Chapelain, you whose violin of such discordant and barbaric memory rasped out its story so crudely under a [rain-] bow cursed by Apollo.)

The pastoral craze – and the resulting popularity of the hurdy-gurdy – lasted right through the eighteenth century. Joseph Haydn actually write concertos for the instrument and dedicated them to the King of Naples, who was a keen player. In this case, though, it was a *vielle organisée*, a hurdy-gurdy to which small organ pipes and a bellows device had been added [figure 117]. During this century there were numerous highly-gifted professional hurdy-gurdy players. While Louis XIV was still on the throne aristocratic enthusiasm was directed towards

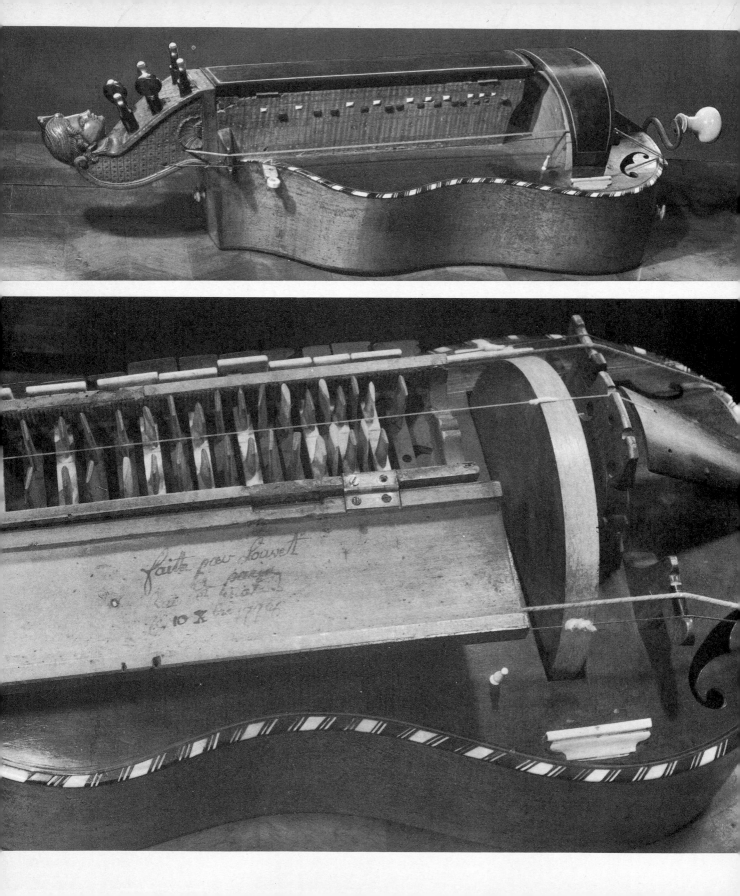

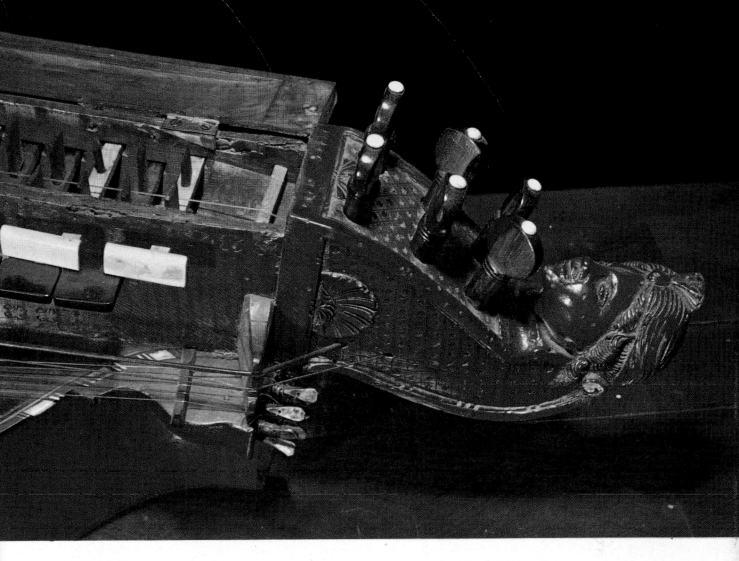

115   Detail of the hurdy-gurdy by Pierre
Louvet [figure 113], Paris, 1770. View into the
tangent-box and of the attractively shaped
peg-box which terminates in a woman's head.
The refined finish of this instrument corresponds
to the high social status of the hurdy-gurdy
among eighteenth-century amateurs.

113   *(opposite top)* Hurdy-gurdy in guitar shape
(vielle en guitare) by Pierre Louvet, Paris, 1770.

114   *(opposite below)* In the tangent-box the
tangents can be moved to left and right to correct
the tuning. The string in play is surrounded by
cotton wool in order to improve the tone. Inside
the lid the handwritten signature is clearly
visible.

the virtuosi Janot and La Roze. Under Louis XV the big name
was Baton, who also left his mark as a composer.

Needless to say, there was always a certain amount of op-
position to the instrument on account of its nasal, rasping tone,
together with squeaks and other incidental noises. One worthy
ecclesiastic, the Abbé Carbassus in his *Lettre sur la mode des
instruments de musique* (1739), described it as a 'permanent
charivari to which is added an accompaniment of croaking frogs
and, in the bass, the hissing or rattle of a knife-grinder's wheel'.

One of the most famous makers was Pierre Louvet of Paris who
was known as the 'Stradivari of the Hurdy-Gurdy'. An attractive
example of his work is in the author's collection. The instrument's body is similar to that of a guitar. The two melody strings
(chanterelles) are, as usual, in the middle. On either side, and
out of reach of the keys, are two drone strings (termed, respec-
tively, *trompette, mouche, petit bourdon* and *grand bourdon*)
which can either be made to play or else be shifted out of contact

116 Beggars quarreling. In the sixteenth and seventeenth centuries the hurdy-gurdy was looked on as a lyre for beggars and peasants. Etching by Jacques Bellange.

117 *Vielle organisée* by César Pons of Grenoble, late eighteenth century, which produces both string- and pipe-music. A bellows serving the two ranks of pipes is concealed in the deep, guitar-shaped body.

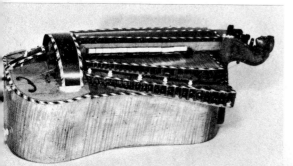

with the turning wheel. In addition there are six sympathetic strings, an innovation suggested by Baton to improve the tone. With its twenty-three key-tangents the instrument has a full chromatic compass of two octaves. Inside the lid of the tangent-box the instrument is signed (by hand): *faitte par Louvet à Paris Rue St Martin le 10 Xbre 1770* [figures 113–115].

During the subsequent Napoleonic era the passion for Roman antiquites assumed exaggerated proportions and spread, occasionally, into the field of Egyptian antiquities (thanks in part to Bonaparte's Egyptian campaign). The light-footed elegance of eighteenth-century Classicism began to assume solemn weight. Dark woods such as mahogany and palisander were given preference; heavy gilt-bronze ornamentation was added; classical designs and emblems were slavishly copied. These trends were felt until the middle of the nineteenth century, and were even partially revived in the latter part of the century during the *Second Empire*. In this late Classicist period it is hardly possible to find corresponding musical developments, although the instruments of the time were affected, outwardly at any rate.

A typical example of the *Empire* style is the PEDAL PIANOFORTE in the Collection of Old Musical Instruments in the Vienna Hofburg Palace. If was made by Joseph Brodmann around 1815. The actual case is hardly distinguishable from an eighteenth-century pianoforte. Both have the same calm simplicity of outline. The glowing palisander veneer, though, hints at the heavy ostentation that was gaining ground. Typical *Empire* accoutrements are the bronze frieze above the keyboard (with bacchantes flanking the lyre-playing Apollo), emblematic reliefs in bronze at the two ends of the keyboard, and decorative bronze mouldings along the fillets. The music stand is topped with a triangular plaque bearing a personification of the sun. The legs are conceived as pseudo-Egyptian *herms* with naturalistic sandaled feet [figure 118].

Joseph Brodmann, born in Prussia, came to Vienna at the age of twenty-five and is considered to have been one of the best pianoforte builders in the Austrian capital. In 1828 his workshop was taken over by his apprentice-pupil Bösendorfer. To this day Bösendorfer pianos remain the leading Austrian make. Carl Maria von Weber treasured a Brodmann pianoforte which he bought in Vienna in 1813 and rated it much higher than instruments by makers such as Schanz, Walter and Wachtl.

Our instrument – from Schloss Wetzdorf (near Hollabrunn in Lower Austria) – is also a pedal-pianoforte, that is to say the normal instrument (with keyboard for fingers) stands on top of second instrument (with keyboard for feet, operated like the pedals of an organ). This application of a pedal mechanism to a stringed keyboard instrument can be shown to begin in the fifteenth century, and the tradition is maintained until the early days of the piano. Mozart, wishing to extend the bass range of his Walter pianoforte, had a *fortepiano pedale* made, and used it for public performances of his Fantasias. As one German chronicler put it: 'many musical works, the could otherwise only be played with the accompaniment of another instrument ... can easily be arranged so that the pedal can replace the second instrument'. Schumann composed special Studies and Sketches for the pedal pianoforte (op. 56 and op. 58) in 1845.

Another prominent instrument-maker in early nineteenth-century Vienna was Conrad Graf, born in Württemberg and brought up as a carpenter. At the age of seventeen he came to Vienna and learnt to build pianofortes with Jakob Schelkle in what was then the suburb of Währing. By 1804 he had opened his workshop and soon achieved considerable fame. Around 1835 his factory was known as 'the largest and most renowned

118 Pedal pianoforte by Joseph Brodmann, c. 1815. By the beginning of the nineteenth century Classicism had assumed a heavier, more solid appearance. The main part of this instrument stands on top of a second case whose 'keys' are operated by the feet. The leather-upholstered bench which forms part of the instrument has 'Egyptian' and 'Roman' elements in its design; the back-rest is formed by a lyre flanked by two eagles, finished in green and gold.

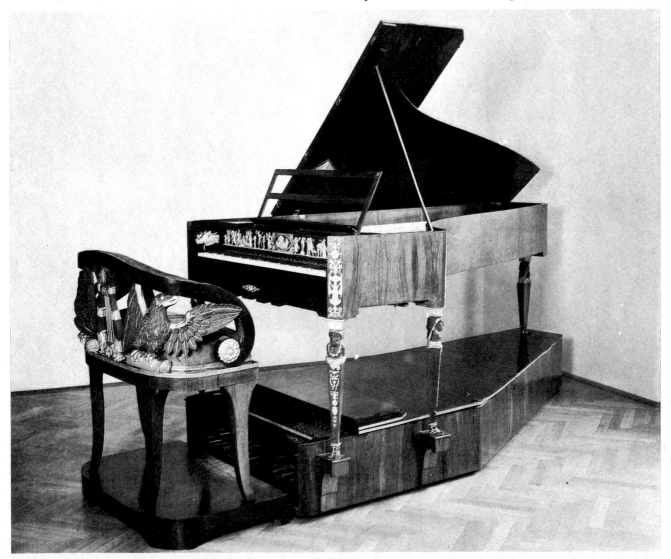

in Vienna and the Empire'. The noble tone of his instruments, singing and poetic, is ideally suited for keyboard works of the Romantic period by composers such as Beethoven, Schumann and Chopin. Graf, who was supplier to the court of Vienna, made an instrument specially for Beethoven. Chopin and Liszt played on his pianofortes. In 1840 he dedicated an instrument to the virtuoso player Clara Wieck on the occasion of her marriage to Robert Schumann. This was later acquired by Brahms who gave it to the Society of the Friends of Music in Vienna in 1873.

A PYRAMID PIANOFORTE from Conrad Graf's workshop, with lavish decoration in *Empire* style, can be seen in the Gemeentemuseum at The Hague. The pyramid pianoforte was invented in 1745 by Christian Ernst Friederici, an instrument-maker in Gera, then a princely residence in Thuringia. This upright pianoforte was presumably built mainly for space-saving reasons (in the same way as the clavicytherium). In the nineteenth century it probably owed its popularity to the decorative effect of its triangular or lyre-shaped body.

The pyramid pianoforte in The Hague [figure 119] was ordered by a Hungarian magnate in 1829 who emphasized that it was to be 'unusual and, above all, a display piece'. Later it was given to one of the servants as a reward for faithful services. In due course the instrument then passed to a village-schoolmaster, before landing up in a junk-room. It had been made by Conrad Graf who is described on the plaque as 'Imperial-Royal Court Pianoforte Maker in Vienna next to St Charles' Church'. The stringing is in a pyramidal case with stepped top which is crowned with an 'antique' urn. The front of the case is adorned with coloured carving in relief. Perched on the then-obligatory lyre is the double-headed eagle of the Austro-Hungarian monarchy, over which hover a laurel wreath and crown. On either side there are pseudo-Egyptian Negro slaves carrying dual-flamed candelabra. Below there are pilasters shaped like Negresses. The extravagant décor is rounded off with numerous bronze ornaments and figures.

The decorative shape of the ancient Greek LYRE, or CITHARA, has always been imitated. In itself it was taken to be symbolic of Music; Apollo was regarded as its most illustrious player. In the early Middle Ages it was sometimes seen in King David's hands in place of the harp. Right up until the twentieth century we still find the shape being used – by piano-makers for the frame of their pedal structure.

Towards the end of the eighteenth century a lyre-shaped guitar was being built in France and, later, elsewhere in Europe. Its outwardly decorative qualities no doubt accounted for its popularity among the gentle sex, although it was in other respects – stringing, fingerboard and playing – identical with a normal guitar. A not-so-distant relative was the HARP-LYRE, an

119 Pyramid pianoforte by Conrad Graf, 1829.

120 Combined music stand for four players, Italy, mid-eighteenth century. The paintings show two horns and two violins.

outstanding example of which is in the Metropolitan Museum of Art in New York. It was made early in the nineteenth century by Carlo Scalfi of Italy. It is, visually, one of the loveliest instruments in *Empire* style that we know. The harp-lyre rests, supported by two gilt sphinxes, on a rectangular base from which, if necessary, it can be separated. This, too, is a classical feature which can be seen in conjunction with lyres depicted on the sides of Greek sarcophagi. The base, which stands on lions' paws, is adorned with Roman relief portraits, medallions with gilt garlands, and the heads of lions. The face of the soundboard is painted with flowers, butterflies and pictures of the Muses. The three sound-holes and the edge of the soundboard have mother-of-pearl purfling. On either side of the yoke is a delicate relief of a winged, torch-carrying Cupid [figure 102].

Also occasionally, although incorrectly, referred to as a 'lyra' is the TURKISH CRESCENT or JINGLING JOHNNY (as it is called

in British military bands) whereby the little bells that constitute its essential element have more than a purely aesthetic function and still exercise some of the mystical magic invariably associated with bells in many different religions. Even today bells affect us in a very special way. The tolling of a large bell has something undeniably menacing about it. The tinkling of small bells reminds one of the recondite aura of widely varying creeds. The Turkish crescent consists of a carrying pole with several arms from which hang tiny bells, cymbals and other tinkling devices. By shaking the pole, or merely by walking along with it, the whole thing begins to jingle. Although the Turkish crescent has been known in Central Europe (thanks to the janissary bands) since the sixteenth century at the latest, it only spread to the rest of the Continent after 1800 when it was adopted by the French Imperial Guard, doubtless in imitation of the ensigns of authority carried in Roman times. A particularly fine Turkish crescent is owned by the Boston Museum of Fine Arts. Although made in Belgium, around 1800, it has the typical Turkish sickle-moon at the top, and its little brass stars stress the oriental character of the instrument [figure 121].

Musickbanda des zweiten Infanterie Regiments in Wien.

Conclusion

121 *(opposite, left)* Turkish crescent from Belgium, *c.* 1800. Idiophones like this have never entirely lost their original magical associations, and more than any other instruments they remind us to this day that music has more than a purely aesthetic function to fulfil.

122 *(opposite, right)* Band of the Second Infantry Regiment in Vienna at the beginning of the nineteenth century; both soldiers wear impressive feathered helmets. The Turkish crescent is built up of several arms with little bells and jingles, and is topped with the double-headed eagle of the Austrian monarchy.

123 *(following page)* Spinet by Arnold Dolmetsch, decorated by Roger Fry, London, 1917–18. Arnold Dolmetsch (1858–1940) was one of the most influential pioneers in the revival of old musical instruments. He and his family have made plucked and bowed string instruments and recorders, as well as a variety of keyboard instruments.

INTEREST TODAY IN OLD MUSICAL INSTRUMENTS is stronger than ever before. Whereas they were earlier regarded as curiosities or, at best, as valuable examples of applied art, they are now equally prized as tools to create sound. This trend is naturally accompanied by a growing interest in music of the past performed authentically. Old instruments have regained their status as sound-producing tools, as magical voices speaking from the past.

Numerous professional musicians now specialize in playing historical instruments such as the recorder, the harpsichord, the viol and the lute. Several specialist ensembles devote their activities to the performance of old music on crumhorns, cornetts, dulzians, Baroque flutes, oboes, bassoons and various sorts of historical string instruments. Permanent orchestras have even been formed which concentrate exclusively on the correct interpretation of Baroque music.

Since original instruments can hardly be bought any longer, and museum instruments are seldom playable, there is a great demand for accurate copies. Recorders and harpsichords are already being produced in factory quantities. This frequently leads to the neglect of significant constructional details – such as the material used – in which the slightest deviation from the original specification can result in serious distortion and, generally, deterioration of tonal quality. On the other hand there is a handful of highly conscientious instrument-builders whose products come fairly close to reproducing the sound of the models they copy. In this category might be included: Martin Skowroneck (of Bremen, Germany) who has specialized in building Renaissance and Baroque recorders as well as harpsichords and spinets; Friedrich von Huene (Boston, USA), with his Renaissance and Baroque recorders together with a successful Baroque transverse flute; Carl Dolmetsch (Haslemere, England), viols and recorders; and Peter Kukelka (Vienna, Austria), clavichords.

These efforts are not just an escapist trip into past delights. Much rather do they amount to acknowledgment of the inherent value of earlier achievements. In this they do much to overcome the firm nineteenth-century conviction of 'progress', whose terrible effects we still experience.

95